LONG TERM CARE GUIDE:

Essential Tips
for
Solving the Elder Care Puzzle

KEYSTONE ELDER LAW P.C.

TABLE OF CONTENTS

INTRODUCTION

This book is a compilation of individual articles written for older adults and their family caregivers who are trying to deal with a variety of complex legal, financial and social issues that occur as adults get older and increasingly frail. The articles were written over a four year period by staff of Keystone Elder Law P.C. They were published in *The Sentinel*, a weekly newspaper of Carlisle, Pennsylvania. While some of the articles use terms and speak to issues which are distinct to circumstances in Pennsylvania, on numerous occasions we have been complimented by a reader from another state who discovered one of our articles from an internet search and found it to be helpful.

Although we are an "Elder Law" firm, we have found that families benefit from more than just legal advice when they are trying to plan for the future or solve the puzzle of the long-term care system during a crisis. Decision-making is affected by physical and emotional health, family dynamics, and an understanding (or lack of) about options for care, just to name a few variables. The information in this book is designed to address some of the fundamental and more extensive needs that can arise within families as a loved one's needs begin to change.

Long-term care is not a frivolous or entertaining topic to explore recreationally. If you are reading this introduction, you probably either have a professional interest or are personally experiencing a situation to which this book's title suggests relevance. One of our attorneys likes to say that "the long-term care system is either broken or has not yet been fully invented." A source of positive energy is needed to nourish caregivers to serve the needs of their loved ones. This book will provide you some essential tips that prove to have invaluable utility for your situation. We hope you find comfort as you read it, and understand that you do not need to feel alone on your long-term, elder care journey.

Some of the details within any particular article may become a bit outdated with respect to exact facts from the date that an article was first created. For example, dollar amounts cited in Chapter 5 in relation to government benefits, the analysis of long-term care insurance as an investment, or tax rates probably will change incrementally. Occasionally, a government program will be renamed or slightly modified. Although the underlying concepts probably remain the same, details often do matter with respect to long-term care issues. This book is not intended to be legal advice for your specific situation, or a substitute for individual legal counseling and long-term care guidance.

More detailed biographies of the authors, and extensive information about legal and social aspects of long-term care planning and caregiving, can be found at *www.keystoneelderlaw.com.*

ACKNOWLEDGEMENTS

The contributions of a number of individuals were instrumental in publishing this book. First, we would like to thank the faithful readers of our weekly column in *The Sentinel*, a daily newspaper published in Carlisle, PA. Their appreciative responses encouraged us to continue to write the articles which became the basis for this book. We appreciate the opportunity given by *The Sentinel*'s publisher, Gary Adkisson on behalf of Lee Enterprises, Inc.; and the support of Naomi Creason, *The Sentinel* editor assigned to receive our contributions.

Marcia Nesbit proofread the columns each week before submitting them to *The Sentinel*. Lindsay Kaslow began the process of organization and editing nearly 200 articles, which first enabled the shaping of this book as a manageable project. Allison Nesbit transformed our vague chapter descriptions into illustrations which lend some softness to subjects which are often stressful. Judi Fennell of formatting4U helped us with final layout, and guided us on our first experience through the self-publication process.

Our clients and their caregivers placed their trust in us, and validated the principles in this book by allowing us to guide them through the complicated maze of long-term care. Our experience walking alongside our clients provided a basis for this book to offer practical tips that have proven to be useful. We are grateful for the many long-term care service providers with whom we have cooperated to serve our clients;

and their level of commitment has helped our clients to obtain the best care.

Finally, we acknowledge one another as authors of the individual articles: attorney David D. "Dave" Nesbit, the founder of Keystone Elder Law P.C.; attorney Jessica Fisher Greene, CELA (Certified as an Elder-Law Attorney by the National Elder Law Foundation); and attorney Ryan A. Webber. Karen E. Kaslow, RN serves as our care coordinator, which is the service that makes our law firm different than most others; and she deserves special thanks for ensuring that relevant articles have been created weekly. None of us could have accomplished what this book discusses without the support of other past and present Keystone Elder Law P.C. team members.

AUTHOR BIOGRAPHIES

Dave Nesbit founded Keystone Elder Law P.C. in 2010, after decades of other careers in the public and private sectors. Difficult experiences with caregiving for his parents and in-laws stimulated his calling to serve as a provider of comprehensive long-term care planning and crisis management services for older adults and their families. Mr. Nesbit earned a B. A. degree from Wake Forest University in 1975, a Master's degree in Public Administration from Penn State University in 1982, and a Juris Doctor degree from Widener University Commonwealth Law School in 1995. He is licensed both as a real estate broker and as a producer of life and health insurance. He is accredited by the Department of Veterans Affairs, credentialed as a commercial and investment real estate expert (CCIM), certified in long-term care insurance (CLTC), and trained and experienced in Elder Mediation. He is a member of the Pennsylvania Bar Association, the Pennsylvania Academy of Elder Law Attorneys (PAELA), and the National Academy of Elder Law Attorneys (NAELA).

Jessica Fisher Greene, CELA, is a shareholder of Keystone Elder Law P.C. Her interest in elder law developed while working in a long-term care facility during her undergraduate years. Mrs. Greene graduated in 2010 from The Penn State Dickinson School of Law, and earned a master's degree (LL.M.) in Elder Law in 2015 from Stetson University College of Law, graduating "with distinction." Her CELA credential is a certification as an Elder Law Attorney by the National Elder Law Foundation. Mrs. Greene is accredited by the Department of Veterans Affairs. She is a member of the Pennsylvania Bar Association, the Pennsylvania Academy of Elder Law Attorneys (PAELA), and the National Academy of Elder Law Attorneys (NAELA).

Ryan Webber joined Keystone Elder Law P.C. in 2015 as an associate attorney after five years of legal experience elsewhere, including employment law and litigation support. Mr. Webber earned a Juris Doctor degree from Widener University Commonwealth Law School in May 2010. Mr. Webber is accredited by the Department of Veterans Affairs. He is a member of the Pennsylvania Bar Association, the Pennsylvania Academy of Elder Law Attorneys (PAELA), and the National Academy of Elder Law Attorneys (NAELA).

Karen Kaslow, RN, has been the care coordinator at Keystone Elder Law P.C. since 2013. Mrs. Kaslow graduated from James Madison University in 1990 with a Bachelor of Science degree (BSN) in Nursing, and has over 25 years of experience in caring for older adults in both acute and long-term care settings. She also became a family caregiver after her grandmother experienced a stroke, which added a new dimension to her practice.

CAREGIVING

FAMILY CAREGIVERS

CAREGIVER. Does this term describe you? As a registered nurse, I chose caregiving as my profession. But my understanding of the role of a caregiver changed a number of years ago when I experienced a new perspective as a family caregiver.

While traveling home from a family vacation, the phone call came. My 90-plus year-old grandmother (the only grandparent I had left), was in the hospital after experiencing a stroke. Immediately, medical training kicked in, the questions poured out, and the planning started. The step following her hospitalization was clear—a rehabilitation facility. But then what? She had been living in an assisted living facility, taking care of her own physical needs and only using a walker due to severe arthritis. Suddenly, the situation had changed, and we weren't sure whether it would be temporary or permanent.

The rehabilitation stay helped her begin to learn to live with new limitations but was nowhere near long enough for her to regain enough strength and functionality to return to assisted living. However, the answer that was clear to me and the direction she thought she should go didn't match. I have a great admiration for the selflessness she demonstrated by suggesting that she should go to a nursing home. "I don't want to be a burden on anyone," she said. Knowing that my grandmother did not have a demanding personality strengthened my resolve to bring her home. This was going to be a piece of cake; certainly she would be easier to care for than many of the patients I had dealt with. I had professional training and experience to provide the physical care, my house had a first floor bedroom and bath, and we already had most of the equipment we would need (stored in the basement from my other grandparents, who had multiple needs prior to their passing). I would have to leave my job, but my grandmother wanted to assist us financially (be sure to speak with an attorney about this). Having 7- and 9-year-old daughters to also care for didn't deter me in the least, and my husband was supportive, even though that first floor bedroom was his man cave.

My grandmother required convincing from multiple family members as well as from the staff of the rehabilitation facility, but she did join our household. I proceeded to learn very quickly that caring for strangers and going home at the end of the day is one thing while providing 24-hour care for a loved one is very different.

Caregiving is a concept that has many variables. Caregivers can be younger or older people, medically trained professionals, or anyone off the street. The recipients of care can have a simple single need or can require complex technical skills on multiple levels. The time commitment can be short-term, long-term, intermittent, or 24/7. Regardless of the details, family caregivers are an often overlooked and underappreciated segment of the population. It is easy for caregivers' needs to be hidden in the shadows because of the obvious requirements of the care recipient. According to the Caregiver Action Network, 2 out of every 5 adults in this country (both men and women) are family caregivers, providing $450 billion worth of unpaid care each year. This amount is more than the government pays for Medicaid and twice as much as professional home care and nursing facility care costs combined. Clearly, family caregivers are essential to the health and well-being not only of the loved ones they help but also of our nation.

What happened to my grandmother? I dare say that I did have it easier than many other family caregivers. My mother (her daughter) lived nearby and was able to provide additional support, my grandmother was mostly agreeable, and our situation was only temporary. I struggled daily with the role reversal of being the caregiver for one who had cared for me, with respecting her privacy (as much as you can with someone who can't bathe, toilet, or dress themselves), and figuring out how hard to push the tasks and exercises she needed to do in order to reach her goal of returning to the assisted living facility. She did meet her goal in less than one year. Although she never said it, I believe it was just as difficult for her to accept the care as it was for the family to provide it. Is caregiving at home the best choice for every family? Definitely not. But we can all recognize the oft times quiet but necessary role that family caregivers play.

Karen Kaslow

THE PROMISE

Americans live in a society in which youth is highly valued and many people become uncomfortable when asked to think about or discuss the aging process. News stories about nursing homes generate greater public interest when an unfortunate event related to patient care has occurred or some type of conflict exists regarding long-term care services. These types of stories may lead an individual to briefly consider the possibility of one day needing additional help with activities of daily living and generate a discussion with a spouse or among other family members. These conversations may include the statement, "Promise me that you will never put me in a nursing home." Let's consider the implications of this promise.

This type of promise may appear to be very logical. During free public seminars about planning for long-term care, our elder law firm has asked hundreds of people over the past few years, "Who has as one of your life goals to spend your final days in a nursing home?" Can you guess how many hands have been raised? Not a single one. Since everyone agrees that one's own home is the best place to be, a promise to never admit a loved one to a nursing facility is easy to verbalize when all involved in the discussion are generally healthy and independent. Although it may be easy to verbalize, following through on the promise can prove to be more challenging than one might imagine.

Whether an individual's mental or physical health

declines as the result of a sudden catastrophic event or chronic disease or one experiences a general slowing down due to age-related changes, the need for assistance with the tasks of life will require someone else to become a caregiver. Caregiving can range from providing help with a single task every once in a while to a monthly, weekly, daily, or 24/7 commitment. Caregiving can include a multitude of tasks such as household chores, transportation, scheduling, medical monitoring, and hands-on personal care. Are you ready to sign up yet? Paying bills or driving someone to the store or doctor's office may sound manageable. But how many of us would feel comfortable if asked to bathe a parent or assist them in the bathroom? Since we do not possess the ability to see into the future, we do not know if this scenario might happen. Caregiving often starts out as help with a few tasks here and there, and over time, the number of tasks and their complexity gradually increases. Some people may be emotionally, physically, and socially equipped to provide intense and intimate care for a loved one, but certainly others are not. Factors such as family relationships and structure, stage of life of the care recipient and caregivers, economics, geography, and the actual care tasks all factor in as to whether or not home is a safe place to stay, with or without the help of paid services. Therefore, making such a promise to avoid a nursing home or other care facility, before having the understanding and experience of how life will unfold, is highly unrealistic.

Couples may view the promise as an extension of their vows. After all, didn't they say "...for better or for worse; in sickness and in health..."? The intent behind these vows is to remain committed to each other. Sometimes this commitment involves recognizing one's limitations and responsibly utilizing available resources to make sure the other partner's needs are met. When one partner promises never to place the other in a nursing home, it is often made with the belief that care at home will always be available, more thorough, and safe. The intent behind the promise is to provide the best care possible for the partner. Sometimes, the *best* care is care outside of the home. While the recipient of care may not understand this, it is important for the healthier partner to keep this fact in mind when feelings of guilt for not being able to fulfill the technical wording of the promise are experienced.

Karen Kaslow

CAREGIVING: IT'S A MAN'S WORLD TOO

In our society, the term "caregiver" has been traditionally associated with the role of women. As our older population continues to expand, the need for family caregivers is also increasing, and a growing number of men are taking on the challenges of this role. The prevalence of dementia and Alzheimer's disease in the older population is also a contributing factor. The Alzheimer's Association's 2014 Facts and Figures report identifies men as having a 1 in 11 chance of developing the disease while women have a 1 in 6 chance, resulting in many husbands and adult sons who may find themselves in the role of a caregiver.

Do men and women view, approach, and experience caregiving roles differently? I recently spoke with a gentleman who cared for his wife at home for 13 years after her diagnosis of Alzheimer's disease. Since her passing several years ago, he has continued to attend the support group that assisted him throughout his wife's illness, and has also facilitated a different support group for the last four years.

Personally, Ernie found that his largest emotional hurdle about caregiving was his uncertainty about "whether or not I had the flexibility to convert myself into a nurturer". Accustomed to viewing life in large part from a business-like perspective, he struggled for about a year to develop the patience, gentleness, and hands-on skills required for caregiving. He believes many other men do not view

7

themselves as nurturers either, and therefore may not adjust to a caregiving role in the same way that some women do.

On the other hand, a business-like approach to caregiving does have some advantages, according to a 2012 study by researchers at Bowling Green State University. They described this approach as "block and tackle," in which the caregiver completes one task and moves directly on to the next one. Ernie's caregiving process involved defining a problem or care need, identifying possible solutions, and then trying each solution to see which ones worked and which didn't. If something didn't work, he adapted the idea or discarded it, but tried not to focus on the lack of initial success in managing the issue. His emotions remained "on a more even keel" this way. The Bowling Green researchers determined that while women may by nature or socialization be more nurturing then men, they also tend to dwell on their performance of caregiving tasks, which in turn leads to anxiety and higher stress levels.

Methods by which men participate in caregiving is another area which differs from women. When assistance is needed, the Bowling Green researchers found that men are more reluctant to ask for help than women. Over the years, Ernie also has found that men are of the mindset to hire help rather than learn care tasks themselves, and are quicker to admit a loved one to a facility than women are. A Pew Research Center survey found that caregiving men are only half as likely as women to report that they provide personal care to their loved one. When the need is frequent emotional support, the percentages of men and women who report that they provide this type of care are closer (30% of men to 39% of women). Generally, men also may be more reluctant to participate in caregiving in the first place. Ernie often hears from daughters caring for parents that their brothers refuse to help.

Interestingly, when I asked Ernie whether or not he had faced any discrimination as a male caregiver, he referred to his wife's family's reactions during the early stages of her Alzheimer's disease. His wife's brother accepted Ernie's observations about her behavior as fact, while her sisters tended to blame him for the changes and "accused me of doing something to her." Ernie also had difficulty convincing their family physician that his wife was experiencing changes. This situation may not be uncommon since in early Alzheimer's disease, the symptoms may be very subtle and the affected individual can be very effective at presenting a "normal" appearance for short periods of time.

In our office, we have seen many male family caregivers who are providing various levels of care, from general intermittent oversight to hands-on 24 hour care. They include husbands caring for wives, sons for parents, brothers for siblings, and even nephews for aunts and uncles. The gender of a caregiver will undoubtedly influence one's fulfillment of this role to some extent, but the overall experience of caregiving will depend on many other factors. For both men and women, flexibility and a willingness to learn are helpful characteristics to possess or develop for the performance of caregiving responsibilities. The engagement of supportive services can also help provide greater stability for both the caregiver and the care recipient, and the earlier these services are sought out, the more benefit a family will receive. Just ask Ernie.

Karen Kaslow

CAREGIVING AND PREVENTION OF FAMILY CONFLICT

Most people, when given a choice of where they wish to spend their final days, months, and years on this earth, would choose their own homes. While many care facilities exist, provide valuable services in our society, and are oftentimes appropriate for our loved ones, statistics show that unpaid family caregivers provide the majority of long-term care for our older adults. However, some of these caregivers struggle with conflicts among other family members (often siblings) about the who, when, what, where, and how of caregiving. These conflicts increase stress not only for caregivers but also the recipients of care if the issues/emotions behind the conflicts cannot be openly discussed and dealt with. After all, no parent enjoys seeing his/her children fight. Shouldn't a parent's final years be as peaceful as possible?

The primary method of achieving this "peace" is communication, which should begin *before* there is a need for caregiving. Older adults should discuss their preferences about lifestyle for the remainder of their lives (both healthy/independent and less healthy/more dependent scenarios), beliefs about end-of-life care, and arrangements they have made (such as appointing a power of attorney, funeral/burial plans, etc.) with their children or other younger family members. Ideally, these discussions should take place as family meetings or conference calls so that everyone involved hears the same information at the same time, has an opportunity to ensure an accurate understanding of the stated desires and decisions, and can contribute comments and questions regarding topics that may require further consideration. If an older adult later develops dementia or is otherwise unable to participate in decision-making processes, family members are not left to guess what he/she would have wanted. While it is not possible to consider every possible scenario related to declines in health, general values and goals may apply to multiple situations. Also, siblings will be less likely to argue over the best course of action if they have heard a parent directly express his/her wishes.

During the discussions about the older adult's preferences and plans, individual family members should begin to consider their willingness to participate in caregiving should the need arise. What responsibilities is each member willing and able to accept? Personal schedules, individual strengths and comfort levels with caregiving tasks, geography, and family members' previous roles and relationships with each other will all play a part in determining a plan of care. Don't assume that all family members will view a situation the same way, make similar decisions, or always support each other. Sometimes, it may be necessary to set "rules" related to decision-making in order to avoid duplicating, contradicting, and second-guessing each member's efforts. Without these rules, the stress of a crisis or the ongoing responsibilities of caregiving can become a minefield between family members. The rules may be challenging to follow at times, but the preservation of family unity and optimal care for the older adult are the ultimate goals. With this type of pre-planning, caregiving responsibilities can be carried out more efficiently and effectively, without threat of confrontation when a new decision is made or a task delegated.

In addition to the above discussions, the organization of important legal and financial documents/information and communication about the locations of these items can greatly

11

reduce stress for everyone involved. Attention older adults, do your family members know the names of your physicians, attorney, and financial advisor? What about where to find the deed to your home, title to your car, and key to your safe deposit box, as well as the bank's name? (Hint: Don't keep your original Will in a safe deposit box, since only the executor will be able to access it, and without the Will, the bank cannot identify the executor). If an older adult wishes to keep some of this information private for as long as possible, I would encourage the creation of a master document that identifies as much of this type of information as possible. Nobody can see into the future to determine why and when this information might be needed, but family members should at least know where to find this master compilation in order to best carry out the older adult's wishes and meet any care needs that may arise.

Karen Kaslow

CAREGIVING AND FAMILY CONFLICT MANAGEMENT

Despite preventative measures, there are a number of reasons why conflicts occur when multiple family members are involved in caregiving. Hopefully there is a common goal of meeting an older adult's physical, emotional, and spiritual needs in a dignified manner and within a safe environment; however, how to meet this goal is where the situation can quickly deteriorate. Each family member will approach a caregiving situation with a unique viewpoint based on personal beliefs and experience, past and present roles within the family, and current life situations. Even families who have always had strong relationships can experience tension when faced with the responsibilities of caregiving.

One conflict that a number of adult children voice is the unwillingness of their siblings to "step up to the plate" and do their parts in assisting with caregiving tasks. Although nobody can be forced to participate in caregiving, there are ways to approach the situation which are more likely to gain greater cooperation. Begin by making sure that all family members have an accurate understanding about the care needs of the individual. Older adults may paint a different picture of how they are doing depending on which family member they are speaking with. To solve this issue, try to reference objective information from third parties (such as a physician, close friend, or neighbor) so that there is more "evidence" to support the need for care than simply the older adult's self-report or primary caregiver's opinion. Based on this information, allow all family members an opportunity to suggest solutions to care needs and carefully consider each suggestion. Perhaps a suggestion may not be the way the primary caregiver would handle that particular need, but, if the suggestion is a safe alternative and the one who made the suggestion is willing to participate in that area, isn't it worth a try? Greater cooperation will occur when others feel that they have been involved in the planning process as opposed to being excluded. When a caregiver answers, "I already tried that" or "It won't work", he or she is sending a message that help isn't really wanted.

It is also important to consider each member's relationship with the one who needs care, as well as with other caregivers. If one child has historically been more distant with a parent than the others, asking him or her to spend one-on-one time with the parent or perform intimate tasks is probably not the best idea. Perhaps less directly-involved but no less important tasks, such as assisting with finances or grocery shopping, would be a good way for this type of individual to stay involved. A potential trap for families is adult siblings to reverting back to childhood roles and expectations of each other. These old roles most likely will not work for caregiving, but acknowledging them may help family members understand each other's behavior. This insight is the first step that leads to changes which can preserve relationships and promote teamwork for meeting the current needs of the elder. Watching a senior family member reach the end of life is certainly not an easy process, and the emotions and reactions of individual family members will naturally vary. If a primary caregiver tries to make others feel guilty about their emotions or levels of involvement, discomfort and defensiveness will follow instead of cooperation.

Two methods that caregivers often use to try to solicit

help from other family members are making a general request or trying to give subtle hints that help would be appreciated. Alternatively, the best approach is to make detailed requests for assistance. Instead of asking if someone can stay with the elder "once in a while," ask a family member to set aside a specific day and time, or perhaps a regular bi-weekly visit. Expectations are clearer for both parties when this approach is used, which will decrease frustration and misunderstandings. It can also be helpful to tailor each request around a caregiving task that takes advantage of various family members' strengths and abilities. A family member with young children may have difficulty running errands but can provide a welcome social visit to boost the elder's spirits and allow a little respite time for the primary caregiver.

One final tip for enlisting the aid of others who may be reluctant to participate in caregiving is to start small. Find a task that can have a successful outcome without an extraordinary investment of time or energy, and remember to say thank you. Just as the primary caregiver's routine probably started by doing one or two occasional tasks for the elder and built up over time, it may be easier for a new caregiver to start by just getting his/her toes wet instead of having to take a deep plunge.

Karen Kaslow

LONG DISTANCE CAREGIVING

The job of caregiving often falls on the family member who lives closest to the one who needs care. Sometimes family tensions develop towards those who live farther away and are perceived as unable to participate. Those who live farther away may develop feelings of guilt or anxiety when they want to provide assistance but aren't sure what they can do. However, caregivers include not only the people who provide hands-on care but also those who perform *any* of the tasks that an individual cannot complete independently. The successful sharing of caregiving responsibilities between local and distant caregivers is possible and can help reduce some of the stress of the primary caregiver.

The first step to long distance caregiving is an understanding of the individual's situation and needs. Schedule a visit with the individual that spans several days so that you can observe how the person makes decisions, solves problems, and completes daily tasks, as well as the roles of any other caregivers. There are many needs and malfunctions that can be covered up for a couple of hours during a short visit, but the observation of overall daily functioning for several subsequent days may reveal significant differences from the verbal reports that the individual provided. Speaking with other family members, neighbors, and friends about their observations of and communications with the individual can also help provide a more complete picture of reality. Researching the individual's medical diagnoses and medications will also promote an understanding of how chronic conditions and their treatments may impact the current and future level of the functioning of the individual.

Is there someone who lives nearby and is already providing some assistance with care? Communicate with this caregiver and find out if additional help is needed or wanted, and what specific tasks are open for negotiation. Good intentions can create bad feelings, and misunderstandings can easily occur when assumptions are made about the caregiver or recipient of care by someone who desires to "help."

What types of assistance can a long-distance caregiver contribute? Here are some suggestions:

- Emotional support for the recipient of care is valuable. A routine telephone call to the individual promotes social engagement and a sense of connection despite physical distance.

- Emotional support for the caregiver is vital. Regular contact with the caregiver reinforces your interest in the situation and allows an opportunity for the caregiver to vent frustrations, share successes, and ask for assistance to problem-solve. Remember to express appreciation routinely and offer reassurance when needed. Avoid "second-guessing" the primary caregiver.

- Coordinate your visits so that you can attend medical appointments or so the primary caregiver can take time off for vacation or personal needs.

- Financial management is an activity that can be handled regardless of physical proximity. A long distance caregiver can arrange and monitor online bill payments, manage banking and insurance needs, complete tax returns, and more.

- Online research of medical issues, identification of local resources for the individual and caregiver, checking equipment needs, comparing costs for professional care (if needed), and investigating types and eligibility requirements of various public benefit programs are examples of assistance which may be helpful as a way to share caregiving tasks.

- Communication coordination also can be done from a distance. Are there numerous family members and friends who desire regular updates? Being the main point of contact can help prevent a primary caregiver from having to repeat the same information multiple times when a change in condition occurs.

The National Institute on Aging has numerous publications that contain valuable information for both local and long distance caregivers. Visit *www.nia.nih.gov* and click on "Health & Aging" and "Publications." Whether you are just beginning or are a seasoned caregiver, the complexity of caregiving can be overwhelming. These free resources can help families understand the emotions and practical issues of caregiving and begin to get organized.

Karen Kaslow

The Increasing Relevance of Elder Mediation

A 2014 report of the Alzheimer's Association includes 90 pages of facts and figures documenting the increasing prevalence of Alzheimer's disease and other causes of dementia. One in nine Americans over age 65 has Alzheimer's disease, which causes somewhere in the range of 60 to 80 percent of all dementia. The benefit of mediation to resolve family disagreements among siblings about the best interests of affected parents is increasingly recognized.

When a loved one suffers from dementia, behavioral changes often create frightening and dangerous circumstances. Unsafe driving, confusions about medications, uncharacteristic emotional or physical spousal abuse, or wandering away from home are not unusual occurrences. Legitimate safety concerns arise, both for the individual suffering from dementia as well as for caregivers and others who could be affected. Lifestyle changes can be legally complicated and emotionally difficult.

If family members are unable or unwilling to make changes to manage the behaviors that arise from dementia, at a certain point, the police and Office of Aging sometimes get involved. When an older person becomes the responsibility of a public agency, a guardianship action often results. This can lead to involuntary placement in a licensed and secure long-term care facility, which might not be the family's preferred option. In turn, sometimes the threat of such outside intervention is enough to get family members focused on the need to make tough decisions.

When family disagreements are addressed in court proceedings, a judge must decide who would be the better guardian for a parent whom is no longer able to act independently. The need for a guardianship appointment is most common when an adult with dementia failed, when competent, to execute a power of attorney document, appointing an agent to act for him/her. A guardianship may also be necessary if no backup agent was appointed to succeed the only appointed agent whose status changes or who becomes unable to fulfill the role.

Senate Bill 568 was recently proposed as legislation which would amend Title 20 of the Pennsylvania Consolidated Statures to make a number of changes to the way guardianship matters are managed by Orphans Courts in Pennsylvania. The proposed legislation introduces the terms "mediation" and "arbitration" for the first time as codified options in relation to a guardianship process. However, elder mediation has existed for many years in some localities.

The Good Shepherd Mediation Program of Philadelphia was established in 1984 and offers both mediation services for families as well as training for professionals interested in providing elder mediation services. Typical elder mediation issues include living arrangements, driving, property maintenance, care issues, and finances. Depending on the circumstances of a family conflict, a mediation session might include three generations of a family, religious advisors, friends, neighbors, service providers, and financial and legal advisors.

Mediation is different than arbitration, in which a neutral party or panel hears a dispute between parties and renders an opinion that could have legal significance. Mediation is a dispute resolution process which participants must approach voluntarily and work through in good faith. A successful mediation hears the wishes of the older adult and encourages family members to work through their different perspectives. Ideally, a mutually agreeable resolution about a necessary decision results from the process of gathering information and considering options.

Some mediators suspend judgment and serve reflectively as facilitators; other mediators are directive and arrange a resolution. Sometimes predicting what result might occur if a dispute would proceed to litigation can motivate parties to reach agreement. A mediator may need to help a family work through sibling rivalries and minimize the current relevance of previous family conflicts and pain.

Decisions about older persons with dementia are difficult. When one spouse equates self-worth with the ability to be a caregiver for the other, this can translate to denial of a need for change. Sometimes, a child who has not been present to observe the decline of a parent with dementia has difficulty processing the significance of his/her parent's decline as reported by a sibling. Mediation can be useful to resolve emotional disagreements about dementia so that they do not get so personal as to create hard feelings, which can permanently divide families.

Circumstances of dementia can create additional stress when family members' disagreements result in tensions which cause relationships to suffer. These tensions, general logistics, and time pressures lead to families avoidance of important and difficult conversations. Not discussing the impact of dementia contributes to a failure to recognize or react to the new reality caused by progressive dementia, and delays important decisions. At least one of the parents might eventually lack the capacity to participate in decision-making about care.

If your family is experiencing the onset and effects of dementia, it is important to attempt to get legal affairs in order immediately. If a consensus cannot be reached about the need to appoint an agent or who should be appointed, mediation might be useful to resolve this impasse. Even if the preparation of legal documents can be completed without mediation, mediation about lifestyle issues could be beneficial.

Dave Nesbit

IS IT TIME FOR A RESPITE CARE "TEST DRIVE"?

Just as many of you have Christmastime traditions, my family always had an elaborate breakfast before exchanging gifts. Christmas morning delighted my mother more than any other time of the year, but I can only imagine how she felt the year she pretended not to notice when my father pointed at her and said: "Who is that woman, and why is she here today?"

I can't recall whether I was more concerned about my father's dementia, my mother's state of denial, their plan to spend three winter months in Florida, my father still driving, or that my mother's knees were so sore she could no longer use the steps in their house. When I visited them in Florida, I discovered that my mother was placing my father's name and address in his pocket before his daily five mile walk, which she encouraged as therapy for his heart, even though he sometimes needed help finding his way home. It can be difficult to persuade parents to make a choice that is obvious to everyone but themselves.

Upon their return from Florida that year, my mother agreed to have long overdue knee replacement surgery. Supportive friends and family members realized that my mother's knee surgery was the answer to prayers of concern for the safety of both parents. She agreed to allow my father to spend two weeks in a care facility "until she could come home from the hospital and care for him." This "respite care" opportunity for my father was the first step of my parents passing through their Alzheimer's crisis without a catastrophe occurring, such as causing an auto accident that might have injured an innocent person.

Your family's circumstances don't need to be quite this dramatic to consider respite care. Many extended care facilities offer temporary, short-term arrangements. The families of our clients have been delighted when, during such a "temporary time", their parents adjusted nicely to their new living environment. If a medical need for a caregiving spouse does not exist, other reasons can be used by your family to "test drive" a personal care or nursing home by using respite care.

In one example, an only child and her husband approached us in desperate need of a vacation after having her mother live with them for a period of time. Although the mother's dementia had worsened and her behavior had become more challenging to manage, the mother continued to believe she was fine. Her daughter knew that she should not be left alone during the two weeks of a long-awaited cruise vacation. We helped them place the mother in respite care at a Personal Care Home, where they knew she would be safe while they were gone.

Our care coordinator checked on their mother while they were gone, and we promised to let them know if issues required their communication. But much like I advised mothers whose Tenderfoot Boy Scouts were attending summer camp for the first time, I asked the daughter not to contact her mother until we advised that it would be appropriate. This allowed a settling-in time for her mother to adjust to the care facility.

Upon their return from the cruise, they were comforted to learn that the mother had participated in activities and had stopped asking about them on a daily basis after the first week. We suggested that they visit her but not bring her home no matter what might happen during that visit. Instead, we suggested that they excuse further delay due to a plan to repaint the mother's area of the house. Two weeks later, the mother came to the house for dinner, with the understanding that they would be taking her back to "her new home" after dinner. While helping her daughter wash the dishes, the mother admitted that she felt a bit confused and uncomfortable in the kitchen and indicated her satisfaction with her new living arrangements.

In the best case scenario, mom and/or dad will agree to stay in the Personal Care Home after their children return from vacation. We often help families with a wartime veteran discover how to make these facilities more affordable through the use of a special pension from the Veterans Administration. Most families can make the finances work using home equity or other tools.

An experienced attorney can help you understand the terms of the entry agreement for respite care. Getting ready for the stay in respite care is a good excuse for reviewing the essential legal documents before the parent's condition of dementia worsens to the extent that guardianship might become the only option if documents are defective. It might be helpful to focus on the similarities between your parents attending respite care and children attending summer camp; and in the same context, consider a visit to your elder law attorney as being as wise as obtaining the required medical physical before summer camp.

Dave Nesbit

WHAT CAN YOU DO ABOUT ALZHEIMER'S DISEASE?

Alzheimer's disease is America's sixth leading cause of death. Deaths from Alzheimer's increased 68 percent between 2000 and 2010 while deaths from other major diseases decreased. The number of persons who have Alzheimer's disease is expected to nearly triple by 2050, from 5 million to 13.8 million, causing some public health experts to call the disease an epidemic.

When a loved one shows early signs of Alzheimer's disease, the family should encourage that at least two levels of agents be given legal authority to act on behalf of the Alzheimer's victim for financial affairs and health issues. There should not only be a Will but, more importantly, also a Durable Financial Power of Attorney, a Healthcare Power of Attorney, and an Advance Care Directive, which is also known as a Living Will. Our website has previous articles explaining why those legal documents, which establish "agency", are important for all adults.

A diagnosis of early-stage Alzheimer's disease does not mean that legal documents to establish agency rights and duties cannot be created. A parent who struggles with short-term memory or vocabulary can recognize a need to ask for help, show willingness to delegate authority, and express preference for a specific person to serve as the agent. A family that demonstrates unified support at the time that agency

25

documents are signed is less likely to have a courtroom fight in the future about the documents' validity. Sometimes, an Alzheimer's victim waits too long to prepare legal documents. Other times, one family caregiver will encourage that existing agency documents should be revised to increase his/her authority at the expense of another family member who currently has the authority. In these instances, it becomes more complicated for a lawyer to determine whether a person with an Alzheimer's diagnosis has the legal capacity to sign documents which delegate agency authority.

It could be important to have a geriatric psychologist evaluate the Alzheimer's victim immediately before the act of signing to determine if sufficient cognitive competence exists. The psychologist could also determine whether there is any indication of coercion or undue influence about the choice of an agent. The determination of competency or capacity is ultimately a legal one, which can be supported by medical testimony about cognition. The process of petitioning an Orphan's Court judge to resolve such a dispute can be as expensive and emotionally charged as a child custody dispute. Mediation should be considered as an alternative.

After the basic agency relationships have been established, a care plan should be created. Caregiving for Alzheimer's disease is a marathon, not a sprint. Consideration is needed to stretch family resources and avoid caregiver burnout related to home care and to stretch funds if care in a secured personal care home becomes necessary. Alzheimer's does not always qualify for care in a skilled nursing home, which is the only facility where Medicaid assistance can be obtained.

Long-term care insurance makes a home care plan or personal care home placement more affordable without sacrificing either the economic lifestyle of the well spouse or the intended family legacy. However, once a loved one's medical chart has an Alzheimer's diagnosis, such insurance cannot be obtained. Those with a family history of Alzheimer's should consider insurance as part of their own comprehensive estate plan before it is too late.

Step one of a detailed care plan is the consideration of various options for care needed presently and anticipated for the future. A budget can project how monthly income, savings, and other financial resources, as well as the potential to obtain government assistance, can meet the current and probable future costs. This plan should be available to any involved family member as well as to other advisors such as an accountant or investment advisor.

Family caregiver agreements build from the care plan and provide a legal way to transfer money from an Alzheimer's victim to the family. A total of more than $500 of transfers in any month from an Alzheimer's victim to family caregivers should be reported to the IRS as a taxable event necessitated by the care plan. Otherwise, money transferred within the family can be considered as a gift and can create a period of ineligibility for Medicaid assistance, which is often eventually needed to the pay the $9,000 per month cost of a nursing home, which is not covered by Medicare. Wartime veterans and surviving spouses may also be able to receive special pensions to help offset the cost of Alzheimer's care. Estate planning techniques should be discussed with an attorney to determine the most appropriate methods of paying for Alzheimer's care.

Dave Nesbit

27

SENIOR CARE AND TECHNOLOGY

In this day and age, there are many ways to stay organized and access information to provide efficient and effective care for loved ones. Whether your loved one lives with you in the same house or across the country, advances in technology now provide individuals still at home with a variety of methods to obtain, record, and share both medical and nonmedical information with their caregivers. Tools also exist to help individuals complete daily "medical" tasks and thus maintain and improve their safety and general health; an introduction to some of these tools follows.

Do you know an older adult who is apprehensive about using technology due to a lack of knowledge or a fear of the unknown? Check out Generation Connect *(www.gen-connect.com)*, a local company that "seeks to bridge the gap" between younger family members who are tech savvy and older ones who may be reluctant to try technology. The company focuses on the use of iPads because they are portable, secure, user-friendly, and easily customized to an individual's wants, needs, and interests. Personalized training is provided by written guides, instructional videos, and hands-on workshops. It's never too late to learn something new!

One of the most basic factors in how stressful we perceive our lives to be is how we manage information. Every day, we are bombarded with information, which can be useful or not, new or old, and simple or complicated. Caregivers face an additional challenge as they try to manage information not only for themselves but also for their loved ones. Keeping things in their heads, journaling, or making To-Do Lists on paper may work for some people. Others may find various apps for their mobile devices a more efficient method of keeping track of contacts, appointments, medications, general tasks, medical diagnoses, communications, etc. There are a multitude of general task management apps available, but some exist that are designed specifically for caregivers. Two of these, *www.carezone.com* and *www.unfrazzledcare.com*, are free and focus on organizing, managing, and sharing tasks/ information. A number of apps specifically for managing medications also are available, ten of which are described briefly on the site *www.nannyjobs.net.*

Accurate medication administration is a common issue for many older adults. One statistic states that, in people over the age of 65, 30 percent of all hospital visits are related to medication noncompliance. A variety of products are available to help combat this problem. One unique product is GlowCaps *(www.glowcaps.com)*. These caps fit standard medication bottles and remind folks to take their medications by the presence of light and sound. A microchip embedded in the lid uses the AT&T mobile broadband network to automatically record medication use, order refills, and notify caregivers of missed doses. A monthly service plan is required. Another tool is a medical alarm watch: these watches can be programmed to beep and display a visual message at scheduled times. Be sure to pick a watch that has large enough text for your loved one to read. For those who are hard of hearing, watches with vibrating alarms are also available. E-pill (*www.epill.com*) has a variety of watch styles available as well as a third type of tool: secure medication dispensers. Medication dispensers can be used by individuals who have trouble managing pill bottles or have complicated medication regimens. The dispenser is filled for a period of time (such as weekly or monthly) and is programmed to dispense the medication at specific times of the day. Alarms are available as well as notification to a remote caregiver if a dose is missed. The medication cannot be tampered with once in the dispenser. Dispensers also come in a variety of styles and have different features depending on the individual's needs and abilities.

If your loved one has a chronic condition that requires medical management, remote patient monitoring systems can be used to obtain and track information such as blood pressure, weight, blood glucose, and oxygen saturation. Wireless technology makes it possible to have readings recorded and stored automatically—no more lists on scraps of paper! Caregivers can easily view the data via computer or mobile device as well as receive alerts based on programmed parameters. Is your loved one's blood glucose level too low or too high? Find out right after the check is done. Or was the scheduled check not completed at all? You can receive a notification about that too!

Additional monitoring systems are available to allow caregivers to track activity levels of individuals who may be beginning to experience symptoms of forgetfulness or dementia. These systems can include sensors to detect motion in certain rooms of the house, pressure (such as weight on a bed), room or outdoor temperature, or the opening of household doors/cabinets. A touchscreen monitor in the client's home can be used to video chat between the caregiver and care recipient, track sensor activity, play games to stimulate brain function, provide visual and verbal prompts to remind the individual to take medication (specifying the type of medication and even showing a picture of it), or complete a check (such as a daily weigh-in). All data is stored on an internet care portal for management by a remote caregiver. This is only one example of a type of monitoring system with multiple features and capabilities designed to help older adults remain in their homes.

One of the greatest challenges today in remote patient monitoring is not the technology itself but the cost. Insurance companies may be reluctant to provide reimbursement for new products, leading to fewer customers who are able or willing to foot the bill to see how these innovations can improve their health and empower them to maintain their independence. As with any new technology, costs should decrease as devices become more mainstream. Consumers will need to weigh the desire and ability to remain at home with the support of new technology against the potential costs of both the home technology and a move to a health care community or facility.

The benefits of using technology in home health care and caregiving are enormous. Improved management of information, timely access to specific medical data, tools to simplify health care tasks, and the ability to see and communicate with a loved one can prevent unnecessary hospital and physician visits, save time and money, reduce stress, and facilitate improved health and well-being. Your older adult may be reluctant to embrace "newfangled gadgets", so start with one idea and try to find another older adult who can share a positive personal experience with the product or program. Hopefully, these few resources mentioned can jump start your search for the right technological tool for your needs.

Karen Kaslow

LIFE AFTER CAREGIVING

For those who are caregivers, life when caregiving responsibilities are reduced or end may be difficult to imagine. Caregiving responsibilities may be reduced or changed when the recipient of care moves from home to a care facility. Caregiving responsibilities often end due to the death of the care recipient. Either way, caregivers may experience a myriad of emotions. The variety, depth, and breadth of these emotions will depend on factors such as the caregiver's personality, the relationship between the caregiver and care recipient, and the extent of caregiving responsibilities.

A variety of reasons exist as to why caregivers may have difficulty acknowledging/processing their emotions until after caregiving has ended. The tasks associated with caregiving may be so time-consuming or socially isolating that little opportunity exists to reflect on oneself and seek the support of others. In addition, caregiving may be physically and emotionally draining, leaving only enough energy for activities deemed necessary. Sensitivity to the feelings of the care recipient and the notion that one should appear strong for the rest of the world may also result in a caregiver repressing feelings that may be interpreted by others as negative. The end of caregiving may result in a flood which one former caregiver described as a "fire hydrant of emotions".

Initially, former caregivers may feel a sense of relief that the responsibilities have ended and that now, there is time for themselves. A caregiver named Katy wrote in a blog, "I am only now remembering that I, too, exist as a separate entity". This sense of relief may lead one to believe he/she is being selfish, resulting in feelings of guilt. Caregivers may also question themselves about whether or not they tried hard enough or if they could have done more. When these feelings arise, remember that it is not logical for one to expect to be able to control everything. Nor should caregivers attempt to compare their "performance" to other caregivers. We all have different strengths, weaknesses, and life situations, so these comparisons aren't equitable.

Feelings of grief will be present if caregiving has ended due to the death of the care recipient. Anger may also surface if caregiving responsibilities were viewed as unfair or if one dwells on personal experiences/opportunities that may have been missed due to caregiving. For those who have engaged in caregiving for long periods of time, the end of caregiving may bring feelings of vulnerability. A gentleman named Richard who had cared for his mother wrote: "At first I felt like someone had opened the zoo door and I'd forgotten how to leave my cage. I missed the structure..." Caregivers cannot pick up their lives where they left off when they started providing care. The world around them has changed, and, in all likelihood, they themselves also have changed. Time is needed to process these changes, learn new roles and responsibilities, and evaluate/adjust life goals. Many caregivers believe themselves to be stronger after the experience of caregiving. "You learn whatever you thought your physical and emotional limitations were, and you stretch beyond them to do what needs to be done" (Darren Walsh, 2013).

While some people may choose to deal with the emotions discussed above, others may not. After viewing a movie at a support group meeting, a blogger by the name of Roaring Mouse (*www.Aftergiving.com*) quoted the movie character's distinction between the two approaches as follows:

"Moving On: Means to simply acknowledge that something occurred... but rather than addressing it from all sides, you skip over it and simply consider the item closed.

Moving Forward: Means to accept the event; walk through and address all of its points and, as you move through those different stages (like on a walking escalator), you eventually move forward into the next item that comes up".

The life of a caregiver after caregiving ends will be influenced by which of these paths the individual chooses to follow. Physical factors, such as the former caregiver's age and state of health, will also play a role, as will social connections and spiritual beliefs. Obviously, life after caregiving for an older spouse/sibling will look very different from the life of an adult child. Regardless of who the caregiver is and the details of a caregiving situation, complex issues can be present, not only during the caregiving phase, but afterward as well.

Karen Kaslow

CARE SERVICES

Demystifying Long-Term Care

Our office often receives calls from individuals who have mature loved ones in need of assistance with their daily routines. Often, these callers are unsure of the types of services which are available, the costs involved, and potential public benefits to help pay for services. Following is an introduction to long term care services.

CARE AT HOME: Services available to those living at home are varied.

Home Care Agencies provide non-licensed staff to assist individuals with transportation, light housekeeping, companionship, meal preparation, errands, medication reminders, and personal care tasks such as bathing, dressing, and toileting. This type of non-medical care is usually private pay, although it may be covered by some long-term care insurance policies. Medicare does not pay for care at home which is needed on an ongoing basis. The average cost of this type of service ranges from $20-$25/hour in our area.

Home Health Agencies provide licensed nurses and therapists to meet an individual's health needs, and sometimes nursing assistants to meet personal needs as well. Agencies are able to bill Medicare and private insurance companies for the services they provide as long as certain qualifications are met. These services are designed to be short-term and intermittent.

37

Waiver Programs are available through the Office of Aging which can provide limited assistance to qualified individuals who are living at home. Call your local county office for additional information.

Adult Day Services are programs which allow adults who have care needs to live at home, but receive physical care and socialization at a central location during the day. These programs provide family caregivers with time to manage other responsibilities, work outside of the home, and have a break from caregiving so that they remain physically and emotionally able to handle the tensions created by caring for another adult. Daily rates start at about $40 for a half-day program to $50-$60 for a full day. Rates are determined by the types of assistance which are needed.

LIFE (Living Independence for the Elderly) is an all-inclusive program designed for older adults who require a nursing home level of care but desire to remain in the community. The services provided include medical care, medications, home care, adult day services, therapies, and transportation. This program is only available in certain counties (currently Cumberland, Franklin, and York in our area); and the state has contracted with private organizations to manage these programs. The private pay cost is about half the cost of a nursing home, but Medicaid (also known as Medical Assistance) is also accepted.

Senior Centers do not provide physical care for older adults. Instead, they provide opportunities for socialization, education, service to others, and nutrition for independent adults who enjoy the company of others and may be at risk for isolation. A small daily donation to help cover the cost of the meal may be requested.

PERSONAL CARE/ASSISTED LIVING: These two types of residential care are very similar. A few years ago, the Commonwealth of Pennsylvania instituted new licensing requirements for facilities who wish to call themselves assisted living, and for various reasons, most facilities providing this level of care choose to be licensed under the personal care regulations. An individual may have a private or semi-private room in the facility and furnish it with their private possessions. Three daily meals are provided, as well as help with care needs such as bathing, dressing, and medication management. Social activities and transportation are available. Some facilities have secure memory care areas for those with a diagnosis of dementia. This level of care usually requires that individuals are either independent or only require limited assistance with their physical transfers and mobility. Individuals are considered mobile if they are unable to walk but can self-propel a wheelchair. Care may or may not be supervised by a licensed nurse, and residents may continue to see their personal physician for medical care. The cost for this type of care is about $3,000-$6,000/month, which is usually private pay. Some long-term care insurance policies may cover this cost, and for some wartime veterans and their spouses, a benefit is available through the VA which will cover a portion of the monthly fee.

SKILLED NURSING FACILITY: This is the level of care that most people think of for long-term care. Individuals who require close monitoring of their physical health, or have more intensive daily personal care needs require this type of care. Licensed nursing staff members are present 24/7, and all medical orders must be approved by a facility physician. Many nursing facilities offer short term inpatient rehabilitation services in addition to long-term custodial care. Medicare and private insurance coverage are available for rehabilitation services under certain circumstances, but they **do not** pay for ongoing custodial care. The private pay cost of custodial care ranges from about \$9,000 to \$12,000/month. Long-term care insurance policies will cover a portion or this entire fee, depending on the specific policy provisions. For those who qualify, Medicaid is also available to pay for this type of care.

CONTINUING CARE RETIREMENT COMMUNITY (CCRC): These communities offer various levels of care within the same organization. Individuals may move to a CCRC at any level of care. Those entering at an independent living level usually pay a significant entrance fee and a separate monthly maintenance fee, but are then permitted to remain in the community even if their health declines, moving to the different levels of care as their needs dictate. Even if their assets "run out," the community will continue to provide care. Some communities offer an option to pay a higher monthly fee instead of the entrance fee. Independent living arrangements may be in cottages or apartments, and a choice of floor plans is usually available. Dining services may or may not be included. A variety of social activities are also available.

Karen Kaslow

CONSIDERING A RETIREMENT COMMUNITY

One challenge that families face during the aging process is helping the older generation decide when it is time to move from the family home. Often, I hear, "They'll have to carry me out of my home because I'm not leaving." While the intent might be to leave the home in a hearse, such a stubborn vow can lead to being taken by ambulance to an emergency room and eventual discharge to a nursing home, an outcome that is not what would have been chosen.

Moving from the family home is a decision that is easy to procrastinate making but difficult to execute. Memories seem to be anchors. Sorting through decades of accumulated possessions is a major challenge. As aging homeowners become more frail, the tasks related to downsizing and relocating become increasingly burdensome.

Moving to a retirement community is normally a voluntary choice of a reasonably healthy individual or married couple who have both the desire and ability to continue to live with some independence. Wise persons who plan ahead have many options for retirement living, including "55-plus communities" and "independent living facilities." These options might appeal to those who are hopeful of recouping their equity or who are unable or unwilling to pay significant admission fees. But neither are licensed to offer any care services; therefore, they are not an ideal choice for individuals or couples who hope never to move again.

Continuing Care Retirement Communities, known as

CCRCs, can be a better option for healthy older persons who have adequate financial resources and a desire to choose their final residences. The ideal CCRC offers an array of options which allow residents to initially move in to an independent living situation with the understanding that various levels of care will be available if and when they are needed. This type of flexibility is ideal for a married couple who want to be assured that, should one of them need a different level of care in the future, the other will be able to function with some independence nearby.

There are only 1,900 CCRCs nationally, 80 percent of which are owned by non-profit organizations. Only 10 percent of Americans qualify financially for admission to a CCRC, and fewer than 2 percent of Americans reside in CCRCs. To a certain extent, CCRCs are an exclusive luxury.

There are differences in the entry agreements and options offered by various CCRCs. Often, those entering CCRCs pay a sizeable buy-in fee, which is nonrefundable after five years. There are a variety of ways that a CCRC agreement can be structured, but there is always a monthly fee. The particulars of how the entry fees and monthly fees are established are sometimes referred to as Type A, B, or C contracts. Some CCRCs have moved away from entry fees and charge higher monthly fees instead.

Usually a CCRC will scrutinize an applicant's finances prior to agreeing to admit him/her with the goal that the applicant's money will be adequate to pay through the end of his/her life. Under typical circumstances, CCRCs promise that residents will be guaranteed priority access to nursing care if and when needed and will never be denied service due to an inability to pay. In this sense, moving into a CCRC is similar to long-term care insurance. When the resident's money runs out, care is subsidized by both a benevolent fund and, in many cases, Medicaid.

CCRCs are regulated by various state agencies, including the Department of Health and the Insurance Department. While the Department of Health keeps close watch over the care given, the Insurance Department does not scrutinize the financial statuses of CCRCs to the level one might expect. For this reason, it is important that applicants consider the CCRC's underlying financial strength, which must be disclosed as part of the admission process.

Before making a decision to move into a CCRC, an applicant should be reasonably certain that he/she will not desire to move again later. The opportunity to move into a CCRC where friends are already present can be an attractive consideration. However, it is not unusual for retirees to enter a CCRC from outside the area without knowing anyone; the variety of activities within a CCRC gives opportunity to make new friends and feel a sense of community. The average entry age to a CCRC is 81 years old, which seems almost too late to enjoy all the benefits that it has to offer. But for couples who are reasonably healthy, a CCRC can still be a great solution. If health concerns are evident, other options might be more affordable and practical, especially for dementia, for which some CCRCs are better equipped than others.

It is wise to have a CCRC entry agreement explained by a knowledgeable attorney. The goal should not be to negotiate a better deal; however, occasionally promises made in good faith by the CCRC at the time of admission are different from the terms of the agreement. In those cases, it can be helpful for all concerned to clarify any promises that that been made, as well as to make certain that the CCRC applicants have realistic and thorough understandings of the contract.

For those who have been well-advised as they enter CCRCs, it could be the last time they ever need to seek legal advice. That, coupled with the knowledge that they will be taken care of in the future even if they run out of money, is very reassuring. That's why CCRCs can be better than a 55-plus community or independent living facility for those who can afford them.

Dave Nesbit

KEYSTONE ELDER LAW P.C.

ARBITRATION CLAUSES IN NURSING HOME ADMISSION AGREEMENTS: FAQS

To illustrate the point of this article, consider the following scenario:

Mother's condition deteriorates to the point where she needs 24 hour care in a skilled nursing facility. Prior to being admitted to the facility, the director of admissions gave Son, Mother's Power of Attorney Agent, a stack of admissions papers which included an Admission Agreement and told Son where to sign, as Mother lacked the capacity to execute the documents herself. An Admission Agreement spells out the contractual relationship between Mother and the nursing facility. Son failed to realize that buried deep within the Admission Agreement was a mandatory arbitration clause requiring Mother to resolve any dispute with the nursing facility via arbitration rather than through a court proceeding. The clause probably required Son to initial the provision. However, given the crisis involving Mother and the large stack of admission paperwork, Son likely initialed without reading this provision.

What is Arbitration?

Arbitration is a method wherein a neutral decision-maker selected by the parties determines the outcome of a dispute instead of a judge or jury. A clause assenting to arbitration effectively requires the resident to waive their right to a trial by jury in exchange for what is supposed to be a speedy and cost-effective settlement. These mandatory arbitration clauses are becoming more common in nursing facility admission agreements.

Are These Provisions Legal?

Yes. Provisions in Admissions Agreements requiring arbitration to resolve all disputes are legal. In 2012, the United States Supreme Court held that states could not restrict the enforceability of mandatory arbitration clauses in nursing home contracts. Therefore, nursing homes have the ability to subject negligence claims to mandatory arbitration. Given this power, it is extremely important that individuals signing nursing home admission agreements be fully aware of whether a mandatory arbitration clause is included in the admission agreement.

Are There Common Problems with Mandatory Arbitration Provisions That I Should Understand?

Yes. The problem with these mandatory arbitration clauses is that often residents or their loved ones are required to make a critical decision about their future without really knowing the nature or extent of an injury before it happens. In our scenario, Son was not thinking about litigating a negligence claim against the nursing facility on behalf of Mother when he signed her admission paperwork.

Arbitration also includes additional costs not required in traditional litigation. In addition to hiring an attorney, Mother will also have to pay her share of the arbitrator's fee, which is charged on an hourly basis. The arbitrator's fee may be comparable to or exceed the hourly rate of an attorney. When litigating in court, one does not pay the judge for their time.

Proceedings before an arbitrator are generally confidential and not subject to public record as are proceedings before a court. Nursing home disputes before an arbitrator avoid public scrutiny and can shield patterns of wrongdoing from prospective residents and their families.

KEYSTONE ELDER LAW P.C.

Proponents of arbitration often cite that it is quicker and more convenient than litigation. However, there are fundamental differences between arbitration and regular litigation. For instance, many of the traditional rules of evidence may not apply. Other rights, such as the right to depose witnesses or to seek discovery, may be more limited in arbitration.

Will Arbitration Lead to Greater Recovery?

Probably Not. While arbitration could potentially result in a quicker resolution to a matter, data suggests that arbitration could lead to a less generous recovery by the resident. A 2015 report by Aon Risk Solutions on Long Term Care providers analyzed 2,168 closed claims between 2004 and 2015 and found that there was no money awarded in 27.5% of claims where a valid arbitration agreement was in place, compared with 20.2% of claims in which there was no arbitration agreement in place or the agreement was determined to be unenforceable. Without arbitration, 1.9% of analyzed claims resolved for more than $1,000,000, while only 0.8% of analyzed claims with arbitration resolved for more than $1,000,000. One reason for the higher recovery outside of arbitration is that courts are generally more sympathetic to a resident's claim than an arbitrator.

Are Mandatory Arbitration Clauses Really Mandatory?

No. My advice to Son would be to seek the assistance of an Elder Law attorney prior to signing any documents on behalf of Mother. However, this advice is not always practical. Often a bed at a nursing facility will open suddenly and may not remain open long enough for a prospective resident to meet with an attorney. The important thing for Son to remember is that he is not obligated to sign the arbitration provision in Mother's Admission Agreement. An arbitration provision is not required for admission to a facility. Son can simply skip over this provision or cross it out and it will not affect Mother's admission.

What If I Have Already Signed an Admission Agreement with an Arbitration Provision?

If you or your loved one have already signed an admission agreement with a nursing facility, you should consult with an Elder Law attorney immediately so that you can be properly advised of any rights that you or your loved one may have or have given up in executing the admission agreement. Depending on the agreement and the language of any mandatory arbitration provision, there may be opportunities to rescind the resident's consent to the mandatory arbitration provision.

The admission of a loved one to a nursing facility can be fraught with stress. Remember to stay vigilant and carefully review all admission paperwork prior to signing any documents.

Ryan Webber

FINDING A LONG TERM CARE FACILITY

When family assistance and community services are not enough to maintain a safe environment and meet the care needs of an individual at home, families often begin to look for a care facility. The most appropriate type of facility will depend on the needs of the individual. Personal care homes (PCH) are a good choice for those who are still able to get around, either by walking (independently or with an assistive device), or self-propelling a wheelchair. Folks in a PCH may require cueing and/or physical assistance with medication management and personal care tasks such as bathing and dressing. All meals and housekeeping are provided by the facility. Skilled Nursing Facilities (SNF) provide care for individuals who have more extensive health care needs. Each of these facilities may be freestanding or part of a larger community. Either way, the task of choosing a facility can be daunting. What should families look for in a care facility?

One of the primary questions when beginning a search for a care facility is the cost. In Central PA, the average cost of a PCH is $3,000-$5,000/month. If your loved one has dementia and requires a secure unit, this cost increases to $4,500-$6,500/month. An SNF will run about $9,000-$12,000/month. While these numbers may sound excessive, remember there are costs associated with staying at home also, such as a mortgage payments, taxes, property maintenance, utilities, and home care. An elder law attorney may be able to provide assistance with planning to obtain public benefits to help pay for care in a facility and provide information about managing assets relating to a spouse who will remain in the family home.

A second primary consideration is location. Does your loved one want to stay in the same area where he/she has lived for a number of years or move somewhere closer to relatives who may live farther away? Older adults who have spouses or strong social networks in the community may desire to stay and continue relationships with friends and community organizations. On the other hand, if relatives do not live in the area, a location closer to them may make it easier for family members who wish to visit often and participate in care. Keep in mind that an individual who loves to be outside and has been living in Florida may not do well if moved closer to a child who lives in Buffalo, NY. Carefully weigh the implications of a move for both the individual and family members.

Once the desired location has been decided, families can begin to look at individual facilities. For individuals with dementia, facilities which have secure dementia units should be strongly considered even if the individual does not require that level of supervision at the current time. Choosing this option may save a move later on. The complexity of care which is provided varies in different Personal Care Homes, so to avoid surprises down the road, find out about the types of care situations that a home does not feel equipped to handle, such as when an individual becomes dependent on others for transfers or mobility. Different rates may be charged based on the types of care tasks for which assistance is required, so be sure to review how rates are determined in addition to what they are.

There are many questions that apply when evaluating any type of care facility. Some are listed below as a general guide. They are not in any particular order, and some considerations may be more important to some families than others.

Staffing:

What types of staff are available (licensed vs unlicensed), and how many are scheduled for each shift?

What types of regular and specialized trainings do staff members receive? Observe how staff members interact with residents when you take a tour—are they relaxed and friendly?

What is the facility's employee retention rate? If you have an opportunity, talk to various staff members. High employee satisfaction will translate to improved care.

Building and Grounds:

Is the building clean, without strong odors, and well-maintained? Fancy décor may give a favorable first impression, but try to look beyond appearances.

Are there outdoor areas which allow for activities and exercise?

Is there carpeting in rooms or hallways? Even though it helps control noise levels, carpeting may make using a wheelchair or walker more difficult.

Is there adequate parking for visitors?

Is lighting adequate and soothing?

Is personal furniture allowed?

Are residents able to control the temperature of their rooms?

Daily Living:

What types of programs/activities are available related to your loved one's interests?

Are pets allowed to visit or reside in the facility?

Where are meals eaten, and at what times? Ask to see a menu.

Are specialized services, such as a hair salon, available?

What is the procedure for residents to voice concerns or suggestions?

Are there residents and/or families that you can speak with about their experiences at the facility?

Asking open-ended questions will provide a more detailed picture of life at a facility. Every facility will have its own strengths and weaknesses. What is important is to find the place that will be the most comfortable for the one who requires care. One additional question should be 'What makes your facility unique?'

Advocacy in Long-Term Care

Every October, long-term care providers celebrate "Residents' Rights" month. Any effort to improve the quality of long-term care services for individuals requires that consumers, families, service providers, and other interested parties understand the protections outlined in the federal 1987 Nursing Home Reform Law. In addition, some states have their own specific regulations relating to the services provided in nursing homes, personal care and assisted living facilities, adult day centers, and other types of board and care facilities. Information about and support for these protections is available at the local, state, and national level.

The rights outlined for nursing home residents in the 1987 federal law were designed to ensure dignity, choice, and self-determination for this population. These rights fall into eight general categories, which are summarized as follows:

- Full disclosure—Residents must be notified of available services, the fees for each service, facility regulations, state survey results, and plans for a room or roommate change. This information must be ailable in languages that residents understand.

- Complaints—Residents must be allowed to share grievances with staff, local ombudsman, or state agencies without fear of retaliation. Facilities must make prompt efforts to resolve these grievances.

- Provision of care—Residents should expect appropriate care and be allowed to participate in the planning and execution of this care (as they are able to). They have the right to be informed of any changes in their medical conditions, refuse medications or treatments, and review their medical records.

- Privacy and confidentiality—These are to be maintained during the hands-on provision of care as well as during any discussion or sharing of medical, personal, and financial information. All residents have the right to private and unrestricted communication with whomever they choose.

- Transfers and Discharges—Specific situations are outlined which allow facilities to initiate a transfer or discharge, such as changes in resident condition (either improvement or decline), issues related to the health and safety of other residents or staff, and nonpayment for services provided at the resident's request. Transfers and discharges are expected to be handled in a safe manner, and a resident may appeal the decision.

- Dignity—All residents are to be treated with dignity and respect. They are to be free of restraints, abuse, and involuntary seclusion.

- Visits—Residents may see whomever they choose, including family; friends; personal physicians; organizations providing legal, social, or other services; and representatives from state agencies. They may also refuse visitors.

- Making Choices—When able, residents should be encouraged to make independent decisions about such things as what to wear, who their physicians will be, and activities both inside and outside the facility. They should expect a facility to make reasonable accommodation for personal needs and preferences and allow for the independent management of financial affairs.

On a national level, the Residents' Rights celebration is spearheaded annually by The National Consumer Voice for Quality Long-Term Care, a group that works to increase awareness and encourage the support of the rights of individuals who are receiving long-term care. This group formed in 1975 as the National Citizens' Coalition for Nursing Home Reform when advocates recognized a need for a national organization to focus on improving the quality of care in nursing homes. Currently, the organization seeks to empower consumers to advocate for themselves and also provides support for individuals and entities who assist consumers with this task through education, training, identification of best practices, and discussion of public policy issues.

Karen Kaslow

OLDER ADULT DAY CENTERS

When many families consider obtaining help for a loved one to stay at home, private home care is often the first option which comes to mind. Another valuable service to consider is an adult day center. These centers, which are regulated by the state, allow adults increased opportunities for socialization while providing assistance with personal care and general activities of daily living. They should not be confused with senior centers, which are designed to provide enrichment opportunities for older adults who can function independently. Adult day centers provide care and supervision for those individuals who require the support of others to remain safe throughout the day.

The Pennsylvania Code identifies the goals of adult day centers as follows:

- Improve the quality of life of individuals with functional impairment

- Provide respite for caregivers and clients

- Provide a community-based alternative to institutionalization

- Promote client functioning to the extent of the client's ability

In order to meet the above goals, centers provide a variety of services including supervision and physical assistance with activities of daily living such as dressing, toileting, and eating; nursing services such as medication administration and health maintenance evaluation; social services including communication with families and care coordination with other providers; therapeutic activities (a monthly calendar must be posted); nutritional services such as meals, snacks, and specialized diets; and emergency care.

Appropriate services for each participant are determined in part by an intake screening within sixty days of admission to the program. This screening asks for information including personal identification (address, caregivers, etc.), a social history (hobbies, interests, previous occupation, etc.), physical and cognitive functioning, the use of additional support services, and other data relevant to the overall situation of the participant. This information is utilized to develop an individualized care plan. Care plans must be reviewed and/or updated at least every six months. In addition, staff members are required to write a progress note in the participant's record at least monthly. Participants are required to have an annual physical exam and medical report.

An adult day center is required to be licensed if services are provided for part of a day for four or more clients at the same time who are not relatives of the operator. The license should be posted in a public place within the facility, and annual inspections are conducted by the state to determine if the facility is operating according to the specific regulations for this type of service.

Staffing is one of the areas covered by the regulations. A center must maintain a minimum staff- to-client ratio of one to seven at all times. Staff members are to include a program director, activities coordinator, program assistants, and a nurse. The nurse may be a full or part-time employee of the center, or nursing services may be contracted through a separate company. All employees are required to have a criminal history background check prior to employment. Requirements for staff education and training also are detailed. Other regulations cover general and fire safety, the physical site, overall requirements, program components, and policies related to the daily operation of the center and special circumstances which may occur.

Payment sources for adult day services may be private or through long-term care insurance, VA benefits, or waivers with the Office of Aging. The cost of services is dependent upon whether the individual participates in a half-day or full-day program and the level of care that is required. Generally, fees are less than the cost of in-home care for a comparable number of service hours.

Adult day services, which usually operate Monday through Friday during business hours, can help lighten the load for caregivers who are on call 24/7 and would benefit from some respite time, or who need/want to continue working yet also desire to keep their loved ones at home. They can be a valuable resource in assisting caregivers to manage a loved one's chronic disease or dementia. At the same time, they reduce the risk of isolation for some of our more frail citizens who remain in the community. Should adult day services be part of your plan to care for your loved one?

Karen Kaslow

LOCAL SENIOR CENTERS OFFER MORE THAN JUST A MEAL

Does the name "senior center" conjure up an image of a group of frail older adults having lunch together with a game of bingo afterward? In reality, there is a lot more happening at these centers than just lunch and some chit chat, and the benefits of attending a center are numerous.

Alice, a 78-year-old Carlisle resident, firmly believes in the value of senior centers. She was initially introduced to the Salvation Army Senior Action Center in Carlisle about 4-5 years ago. She had to walk through the center to access the AARP representative who was to help her with her taxes, thought it looked interesting, and asked if she could visit. She became a regular until she lost her daughter a little over a year later, fell into a deep depression, and stopped going *anywhere* except the grocery store. Throughout an extensive absence, the director continued to support her by telephone, and Alice credits this encouragement with making her "more determined to get back to the center." Once her depression was medically stabilized, she returned and now attends five days per week. She describes the center as "her life" and says it "keeps her going." Stephanie and Susan, who manage the program, are her "angels," and she is at a loss for words to describe her appreciation for their genuine care and concern for each individual at the center. But attention from the staff is not her only reason to attend. Alice has developed friendships, enjoys a variety of recreational activities, and has a sense of purpose in being able to interact with peers and help "lift others who are down." Alice's physician has noticed a positive difference in her and specifically asked her if she had resumed attending the center. Alice lives independently, is able to drive, and does not appear "frail" by any means. Although she could choose to participate in independent leisure activities, the center has become her "family", and she doesn't want to imagine life without it.

Oversight for senior centers is the responsibility of local Offices of Aging, and while some public funding contributes to their services, each center is also responsible for maintaining a sponsor and raising some of its own support. Individual centers may vary in their days and hours of operation, the types of programs and services offered, and their size. In general, their focus is on providing:

- Information and assistance
- Health and wellness programs
- Transportation services
- Meal and nutrition programs
- Social and recreational activities
- Educational and arts programs
- Employment assistance
- Volunteer and civic engagement opportunities

The National Council on Aging reports that "research shows that older adults who participate in senior center programs can learn to manage and delay the onset of chronic diseases and experience measurable improvements in their physical, social, spiritual, emotional, mental and economic well-being." The theme for one National Senior Center Month (September 2014) was "Experts at Living Well," and it appears that the Salvation Army Senior Action Center has helped Alice do just that.

Among older adults, reluctance to explore the services of a local senior center may be due to a number of factors. Lack of awareness or understanding of local programs, impaired health and/or functional status, transportation, and lifelong patterns of low participation in voluntary organizations may be some of the reasons why adults who would benefit from senior centers choose not to become involved. The only requirement to qualify for this service is to be age 50 or older. Most senior centers ask for a small annual donation to become a supporting member (the Salvation Army requests $20). Participants can come and go at will, and centers can provide referrals for transportation assistance if needed. For those who wish to eat meals at the center, individuals must be at least age 60, there is a small donation per meal, and meals must be ordered in advance. Daily activities may be organized or spontaneous depending on participants' desires, needs, skills, and interests.

Across America, more than 11,400 senior centers are serving over one million older adults every day. Information about Pennsylvania's senior centers can be obtained from the Pennsylvania Department of Aging website at *www.aging.state.pa.us* or from the county Office of Aging. Are you feeling lonely or bored? A local senior center just may be able to help.

Karen Kaslow

HEALTH

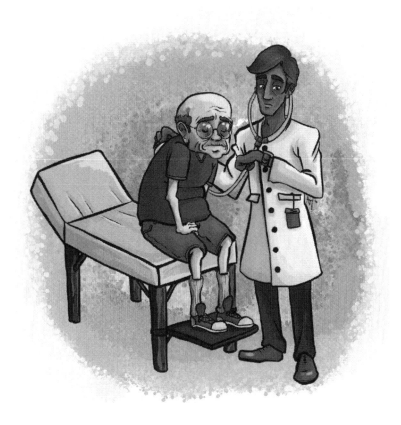

HEALTH LITERACY IMPACTS HEALTH STATUS

In 1992 and 2003, the U.S. Department of Education conducted a national assessment of adult literacy. The purpose of the assessment was to determine not only adults' ability to read, but also how they apply printed and written information to daily life in home, work, and community settings. The assessment focused on three types of literacy skills: prose, which is continuous text (example: a newspaper article); document, which is non-continuous text (example: a job application); and quantitative, which are skills involving numbers (example: balancing a checkbook). All three types of literacy skills are important to possess in order to manage one's health. The ability to accurately complete insurance forms, understand the directions on a medication container, or follow discharge instructions after a visit to a hospital or urgent care center are a few examples of how literacy impacts an individual's health status. The 2003 adult literacy assessment included situations such as these to specifically measure health literacy. The term "health literacy" was first used in the 1970's, and refers to an individual's ability to access and interpret health information which then can be used to make health care decisions.

The Journal of the American Medical Association called health literacy "the strongest predictor of health status" (1999). In addition, while medical care is becoming more complicated, the trend in health care is for people to accept more responsibility for their own care. Therefore, health literacy is especially important for older adults, since as people age, they are more likely to experience one or more chronic health conditions which require active management. Unfortunately, in the sixty-five and older age bracket, only 3% of participants scored in the proficient category of health literacy, while 59% scored in the basic or below basic categories. Overall, older adults scored the lowest of any age group on this portion of the assessment.

Older adults are not the only population at risk for low health literacy. People living below the poverty line, cultural and ethnic minorities, people who speak English as a second language (even if they are fluent), and people with less than a 12th grade education are also at risk. Differences in how these groups of people process and understand health information is a primary component of health literacy, but another component which must be considered is how and why people initially obtain information and then use the information to make decisions.

There are a number of signs which can indicate low health literacy. When people are having difficulty obtaining information, understanding it, and/or applying it, they are more likely to report that their health is poor and verbalize frustration with their health care providers. They are less likely to use preventative services and may have periodic or frequent hospital admissions or visits to the emergency department. People with low health literacy may also have difficulty following a medication regimen and demonstrate poor management of their chronic health conditions.

Health literacy involves more than just an individual's ability to read. When your doctor tried to explain the results of a test at your last office visit, how much of the explanation did you recall after leaving the office? Have you ever had to take a medication where the individual pills didn't come in the exact dose that you were supposed to take? (This is especially true with the blood thinner Warfarin). Have you tried to research a new diagnosis or set of symptoms on the internet, and discovered confusing or conflicting information? Health literacy, the ability to obtain, interpret, and apply information to maximize personal wellness, has an impact on the outcome of each of these situations. Improvements in health literacy can lead to better health. Health care providers as well as individuals can implement strategies to work toward this goal.

The first step toward making these improvements is an understanding (by both individuals and health care providers) of the factors which affect health literacy. To a certain extent, one's level of health literacy is dependent upon educational skills such as reading, math, listening, comprehension, and critical thinking/analysis. But there are also personal, cultural and environmental influences which will have an impact on the successful communication and understanding of health information. A closer look at the obstacles will demonstrate how better outcomes can be achieved by changing our current approach to health literacy.

An initial step toward improving health literacy is consideration of the subject material in relation to the personal and cultural background of the intended audience members. Is information wanted and what are the expectations? Is the information relevant for them and do they comprehend how and why it is relevant? The motivations of the learner will greatly impact the quality of attention which is given to the information. Prior knowledge and experience regarding the subject, religious and cultural beliefs/ health practices, the availability of social supports to assist with learning and reinforcement of the information, and financial considerations are additional factors which will influence the willingness to learn, acceptance of the information, and application of the information.

For example, the educational needs of two people who are at risk for heart disease are much different if one individual was raised on southern fried food and the other eats healthy foods but has a sedentary job. Teaching about the

65

benefits of a certain medication in the management of a disease may be lost on someone whose family member experienced terrible side effects from the same medication, or if paying for the medication is a concern. Finally, how does one handle learning to inject insulin if there is a fear of needles? In all of these situations, a personalized approach to sharing health information can be effective in identifying potential stumbling blocks for the learner so that adjustments to education and a treatment/care plan can be made sooner, resulting in improvements in overall health.

The educational skills, cognitive abilities, and preferred learning style of the audience also must be accounted for when preparing and presenting health information by verbal instruction or in written format. Vocabulary is a major element in these areas, since the practice of medicine has a language all its own. Do you know what a doctor is talking about if he tells you that you had a myocardial infarction? If you fracture your humerus, where is that? Have you ever looked at a written prescription which contained abbreviations like p.r.n. or b.i.d.? When health professionals are sharing information, they must be careful to use terms that will be understood by the general public. If you are on the receiving end of health information, don't be afraid to ask your provider about language that you don't understand. It is difficult to follow instructions or make informed decisions if you are unable to fully comprehend what you have read or been told.

In addition to vocabulary, listening to and reading health information will also be impacted by sentence structure and length, and the organization of the information. Information which is divided into short sections and presented in a logical order is more likely to be understood and retained. Listening skills may be affected by the speaker's tone of voice and accent, and how slowly or quickly the speaker talks. Reading skills may not only involve words but also the ability to interpret diagrams, illustrations, or graphs. The presence of hearing or visual impairments may further complicate the receipt of information. The additional cognitive effort required just to absorb the information can create confusion about facts which might otherwise be understandable. Each of these details needs to be tailored to the abilities of the audience in order to promote successful learning.

Another potential obstacle to health literacy is the type and complexity of health information. Some topics are more highly publicized than others, which may lead professionals to assume mistakenly that these topics are general knowledge and don't need to be reviewed. Other topics may contain highly detailed information, not all of which a learner may need or want to hear. The amount of information that should be presented at any one time may depend on the "wow" factor of the information. When new health information will be life-changing, the first sentence of the communication may be all that an individual is initially able to absorb. Thus, teaching about a cancer diagnosis should be approached much differently than teaching about the benefits of weight loss.

Simple obstacles which may sometimes be overlooked involve environmental factors. Is the doctor trying to explain something to you while you are still wearing a thin paper gown in a chilly exam room? Were you given an informational pamphlet to read while sitting in a noisy waiting room? Are you distracted by news that a friend shared during a phone call prior to your appointment? Did you skip breakfast and now you are expected to pay attention when the lunch hour is approaching? Environmental factors may not seem as important, but they can significantly affect the success of an educational opportunity.

Improving one's health literacy requires an understanding of these educational obstacles, as well as concepts about how people make decisions and the practical implications of applying those decisions to daily life.

A panel of professional experts in the field of health literacy met in 2009 to discuss the status of health literacy among older adults. One of the presentations at this conference dealt with communicating health information in terms of gains and losses and how this communication can influence an individual's decisions about care and treatment. In general, research has shown that if treatment choices are explained according to the benefits a person might gain, the person is likely to choose the "sure thing" or the most predictable option. On the other hand, if the discussion focuses on losses that the individual might experience, a riskier treatment option is more likely to be chosen. When an individual is considering a decision about a specific treatment, it may be beneficial to look at the potential outcomes from both viewpoints. For example, consider a person with arthritis who is considering pain management with medication versus knee surgery. If the physician states that with proper dosages, medication will minimize the discomfort so that the individual can continue to go about their daily routine, this sounds like a safe and reasonable choice. But if instead, the physician states that with only pain medication, the person *might* eventually need to use a walker, does that change how one considers the potential risks of surgery?

Also related to health care decision-making is the frequent presence of a "trade-off." An individual may have to choose whether or not to comply with a treatment that will improve one aspect of health but negatively impact another (medication side effects are a prime example). A second common trade-off is improved health versus financial burden. Will the potential benefits of a suggested treatment outweigh lifestyle adjustments that must be made in order to afford the treatment? In both of these situations, the cognitive skill of understanding probability and risk plays a role, and this skill is one of the most challenging required for health literacy. Many people are reluctant to admit that they may not fully understand information that has been presented, and may answer "No" when asked if they have any questions. Instead of answering "No," the patient should try to rephrase the information that has been communicated by a care provider,

"Do you mean that if _____, then I will _____?" This allows a care provider to assess where there may be gaps in understanding.

Linda Miller, a Community Services Coordinator from North Carolina who was part of the 2009 expert panel, suggested six steps that professionals can take to improve educational interactions with older adults:

- Keep the information focused

- Repeat it as needed

- Allow time for the individual to process the information

- Communication should take place in person, and the information should be relevant to the individual

- Draw attention to the short-term benefits of taking a specific action

- Provide follow-up

Older adults can do their part toward improving interactions with health care providers by taking time to identify and prioritize the issues of concern prior to an appointment. Writing down questions can help organize thoughts and help one get the most out of an appointment. While physicians may not have time to answer every question, they can address the most important ones, and then perhaps nurses or other office staff can spend a few extra minutes covering the remaining concerns. Take time to write down the answers also, as a reference for later on. It is also important to be specific about how a situation is affecting your life. Telling a care provider that you have a pain in your shoulder might get you a prescription for pain medication. Telling the provider that the pain makes dressing difficult and that you are staying at home in your pajamas every day should elicit a stronger response.

Older adults must also be honest with their care providers about the practical application of health information to their daily lives. An individual may understand health information and want to follow through with it, but challenges may exist which will complicate the plan. How much professional support will the individual need, and is this support available in their community? What distractions are present which will hinder compliance, such as family situations or financial concerns? Does the individual have limitations (physical, emotional, or barriers in the home setting) which will impact their ability to carry out instructions or perform certain tasks? Even when health literacy may be limited, individuals can be successful in meeting their health goals when they are assisted to develop "a reliable, sustainable self-care system that is useful in their everyday environment" (Dr. Joanne G. Schwartzberg, American Medical Association, 2009).

Efforts by both individuals and professionals toward improving health literacy can create information that is more useful and relevant, leading to care that is higher quality and more cost effective. The greatest benefit for individuals and society will be better overall health.

Karen Kaslow

THE DANGER ZONE

Obviously, none of us have a crystal ball to see what lies ahead of us. Often, this is a good thing; we don't spend our healthy years fretting over future events that we cannot control. However, it is wise for us to plan ahead for the possibility of becoming frail in our later years so that we can maximize our options and have choices should health care needs arise. There are some steps that can be taken to reduce the possibility of a future health care crisis.

As we grow older, our bodies undergo natural physical changes that affect the way we function. We hope for a very slow progression toward frailty, however, disease processes and lifestyle choices can accelerate the path toward greater dependence on others. The "danger zone" exists in the early stages of health status changes. When individuals begin to require help with routine daily functioning or disease management and they do not receive any assistance, their risk for a more rapid decline or catastrophic health event increases. Remember the old saying "A stitch in time saves nine"? Well, it applies to your health too.

There are several reasons why people do not receive assistance and care when changes in health begin to occur. Some older adults may not recognize their limitations. If the changes occur gradually, people may adapt their lifestyles in small ways without thinking about the long-term effects. Then, a family member or friend who hasn't seen the person in a while visits and is surprised and concerned by the altered functioning. Cognitive changes may also impair an individual's ability to reason and understand that help is appropriate and/or necessary in his/her situation. If limitations are recognized, an individual may not be willing to admit that help is needed for fear of losing independence or placement in a nursing home. Instead, he/she may deny that an issue exists, minimize its severity, try to cover up the situation, or withdraw from contact with those who might address it. Reluctance to receive help may be due to a spouse's belief that, no matter the extent of the care, he/she is the one responsible to provide it since no one else will be able to provide the same quality of care, or that his/her loved one won't allow anyone else to provide the care. Some people may not understand who to call or how to obtain the help that is needed. One final and very common reason for older adults refusing to obtain care or assistance is "It costs too much". Well, if a little bit of assistance now is too expensive, what happens later when a higher level of assistance is needed because complications arise from the smaller issue that wasn't addressed?

Don't let the "danger zone" catch you unprepared—a variety of health assistance options exist. Knowing when and where to get help may make a world of difference for you or a loved one.

Karen Kaslow

UNDERSTANDING ADLS

When the most people consider the concept of long-term care, they closely associate this concept with medical care. This association can lead to misconceptions about where and how long-term care is provided, when it is needed, and who pays for it. Essential to an understanding of long-term care and its components are criteria which, in the industry, are called ADLs, or *Activities of Daily Living*. Identification of an individual's level of functioning in relation to these criteria can help families and professionals determine appropriate types of services and methods of payment for these services.

There are six primary ADLs that are necessary for personal functioning:

- Bathing
- Dressing
- Eating
- Transferring
- Toileting
- Continence

The first three are easily understood. Transferring refers to the ability to move oneself from a bed to a chair, from one chair to another, etc. This skill is used instead of walking (or ambulation) to assess mobility. Toileting and continence may initially be thought of as the same; however, toileting refers to the ability to physically use a commode for elimination while continence is the ability to recognize the need for elimination (bladder and/or bowel) and maintenance of control of the actual process.

There are many other tasks that people perform each day which contribute to health, safety, and the management of personal/social responsibility. These tasks are often referred to as IADLs, or *Instrumental Activities of Daily Living*. Examples of IADLs include housekeeping, meal preparation, shopping, transportation, taking medications, financial tasks such as paying bills or balancing the checkbook, caring for pets, and using a telephone. For older adults, care needs often begin with IADLs.

The provision of assistance with ADLs and IADLs is not considered medical care; instead, it is often called custodial care. For this reason, the cost of long-term care is not covered by Medicare, which is a form of medical insurance. For those who qualify financially, the cost of long-term care may be covered by Medicaid (also known as Medical Assistance), but one must reside in a nursing home to receive fully paid 24-hour care, and a physician and the Office of Aging must verify that the individual requires a certain level of assistance with ADLs.

For those who require minimal to moderate assistance with their ADLs and IADLs, long-term care can be provided by home care agencies, personal care homes, assisted living facilities, and adult day care services. These types of care are usually private pay but may be covered by some long-term care insurance (LTCI) policies. LTCI policies often claim that an individual must require assistance with at least two ADLs in order for the policy to pay for care services. Read the policy carefully, because if the individual only needs assistance with IADLs, the services may not be covered. Also, the type of provider may impact coverage eligibility.

For older adults without the financial means to pay for care, waiver programs exist which are able to provide some assistance. The county Office of Aging will evaluate the individual's ability to perform ADLs and IADLs as part of the application process. ADLs are also taken into consideration for a benefit available for wartime veterans and their spouses. The Aid & Attendance benefit is designed specifically to help cover the cost of long-term care.

There are many details which can influence a long-term care situation. The distinction between ADLs and IADLs is one aspect to consider in order to advocate successfully for a loved one who requires that care.

Karen Kaslow

IS DEPRESSION A NORMAL PART OF AGING?

The process of aging brings about many changes in an individual's health. Decreased muscle strength and flexibility, wrinkled skin, and vision changes are just a few of the common physical changes that occur during the aging process. Cognitively, the mind may become less sharp due to decreased blood flow to the brain, changes in diet, or decreased stimulation. But does depression naturally follow these other issues?

Let's begin with a definition of depression. Depression is a prolonged sense of emptiness or hopelessness and a loss of interest in activities. It may last for an extended period of time and affect an individual's ability to complete the tasks of daily living, or it may be present as a chronic attitude of gloominess while the individual continues to function. The symptoms of depression can include: loss of appetite or overeating; decreased concentration; frequent feelings of irritability, anxiety, sadness, or guilt; problems sleeping or sleeping all the time; difficulty making decisions; general fatigue; and frequent aches and pains. Many of these symptoms can also be the result of other disease processes or the side effects of medications. If an elderly person simply accepts some of these symptoms as part of "getting older," he/she may not verbalize the presence of the symptoms to his/her physician or family members, thus making an accurate diagnosis difficult. In addition, depression may sometimes be mistaken for dementia, due to a similarity of symptoms. A thorough review of the individual's mental functioning can help distinguish between the two conditions. There are a number of factors which can contribute to depression. A family history of depression can lead to a greater likelihood that an individual will develop depression. In addition, differences in brain chemistry or the presence of certain chronic diseases, such as thyroid disorders, may place some individuals at a greater risk for developing depression. Vascular depression is caused by decreased blood flow to the brain due to the stiffening of blood vessels as one ages. The presence of stress caused by life changes is a primary risk factor for the development or worsening of depression in the elderly. Potential stressors include chronic pain or disease, loss of a spouse or close friends, a move from one's home, and loss of independence (such as giving up driving). Whether or not these stressors lead to depression is influenced by the individual's perception of the stressor, ability to cope, and social support system.

Depression can be treated in a number of ways. First, it is important to determine if the depression is related to another illness or a medication. Discuss the presence of ALL symptoms with a physician, whether or not they seem significant or related to each other. In addition, the physician should be aware of all medications that are being taken, including vitamins, herbal remedies, and over-the-counter products. Avoiding alcohol, illegal drugs, and sleep aids can help in reducing symptoms of depression. Exercise can provide both physical and emotional benefits by increasing the presence of certain chemicals in the brain that help one "feel good" and providing opportunities for increased socialization and distraction from negative thoughts. If antidepressant medications are tried, be aware that several weeks may pass before any change is noticed. Counseling or psychotherapy services may be needed if other interventions are ineffective. Often, a combination of treatments is more effective than a single treatment.

So, is depression a normal part of the aging process? NO, it is not. It is important to diagnose and treat depression in older adults because depression contributes to higher mortality rates. In addition, a depressive episode that is untreated or undertreated can lead to a more intense episode of depression in the future. Men who are older than 65 are the highest risk group for suicide. At any age, depression is painful to experience personally or to watch a loved one experience. An accurate diagnosis and compliance with treatment can improve the quality of life not only for the individual but for family members as well.

Karen Kaslow

PILLS, PILLS, AND MORE PILLS

How many pills do YOU take every day? Do you know their names and what they are for? Have you ever changed the dose of your medication yourself (used a little more or a little less depending on how you were feeling)? A large number of older adults take one or more medications every day. As people age, they are more likely to develop multiple chronic diseases which require medication. However, normal aging changes which occur in body organs such as the liver, kidneys, and heart can lead to an increased risk of overdose or side effects. In addition, there are many underlying social issues affecting medication use. So, are medications helpful or harmful? Let's see how you can receive the lowest risk and most benefit from your medications.

When health care providers talk about medications, what exactly are they referring to? The term "medications" refers not only to the pills you take that have been prescribed by a physician but also any vitamins, herbal and dietary supplements, creams, ointments, eye drops, and "over-the-counter" products. When discussing medications with health care providers, it is important that you include all of these products in your discussion. Even products as common as Tylenol can have undesirable or even dangerous side effects when combined with other medications. Also, remember to include products that you may have been using for a long period of time. As we age, the way our bodies process and utilize medications changes, so the medication that you have used for years with no apparent difficulties may still cause issues in the future.

Who is at the greatest risk for potential harm from inappropriate medication use? People who *live alone* do not have another individual immediately present who will notice subtle changes in functioning that may affect or be the result of medication use. Those who are *experiencing some memory issues* may forget to take their medication or may take extra doses. If you *take three or more medications* (including everything listed above), it is easier to get them mixed up, especially if they look similar or have similar names. Multiple medications also increase the possibility of interactions with each other, which may lead to side effects such as physical complaints, decreased effectiveness of the medications, or hypersensitivity to the desired effect of the medications. *Obtaining prescriptions from more than one doctor or filling prescriptions at more than one pharmacy* can prevent the safeguard of physicians and pharmacists screening for potential medication interactions if these health care providers are not aware of all of the medications which are being used by the consumer. Any of the above factors can be experienced by individuals of all ages, but the likelihood of having one or more of these factors present is increased for older adults, making them especially vulnerable to unsafe medication use.

So, what can you do if medication is a required part of your treatment plan? Follow the tips below to reduce your risks and maximize the benefits of your medication use.

- Carry a complete list of ALL of your medications in your wallet at all times. Include the name of the product, the dose, and how often you take it.

- Talk to your doctor or pharmacist if you have financial concerns that may prevent you from using a specific type of medication. Less expensive substitutes are often available.

- If you have difficulty with your eyesight, have someone double check your ability to correctly read the labels on your medication containers.

- Difficulty opening medication containers? Ask your pharmacist about other options for packaging your medications.

- Discuss any physical symptoms you experience with your doctor, even if they seem insignificant. Unpleasant side effects can lead to decreased compliance with taking medications. A change in dose or type of medication may relieve or reduce the undesired symptoms.

- Pick nonprescription medications that treat only the specific symptoms you are experiencing. (For example, if you have nasal congestion, use a decongestant only, instead of a multi-symptom cold reliever containing pain medication or a cough suppressant that you don't really need.) If symptoms worsen or do not go away, check with your doctor.

- Have a new prescription? Make sure you understand the details of it before leaving the doctor's office. Details include the name of the medication, what it is for, the dose, when and how often to take it, special considerations (such as if it should be taken with or without food), and how long you should expect to take it.

- Are you taking too many pills in the morning? Ask your doctor or pharmacist if some once daily medications can be taken at another time of day instead.

- Have trouble swallowing pills? Mix them whole in something soft, such as applesauce or pudding. Some medications may also be available in liquid form; however, there may be a price difference.

- Use a pill organizer if you take multiple medications once or multiple times daily. Organizers come in different sizes and styles to meet your needs, and they can be an easy way to check whether or not you have taken your medications.

- Store medications appropriately. Most should be kept in a cool, dry place (which is NOT the bathroom!). Some may be sensitive to light or require refrigeration. Improper storage may lead to decreased effectiveness of the medication.

- Is your medication regimen too complicated? Check with your doctor or pharmacist to see if the number or frequency of medications can be reduced. A simpler medication routine can increase compliance and positive outcomes when using multiple medications.

Karen Kaslow

MEALTIME CHALLENGES FOR OLDER ADULTS

Over the past few years, much attention has been devoted to the American family dinner, and studies suggest that children and teenagers demonstrate social, emotional, and physical health benefits when their families routinely eat together. Less research has been done about mealtime routines for older adults, although most health professionals would agree that nutrition plays a significant role in the aging process. Both physical and social factors impact an older individual's nutritional status.

There are a number of physical factors associated with an individual's ability to prepare and consume meals. Oral hygiene is a primary factor to consider. The presence and condition of natural teeth or dentures influences the types of foods that an individual may be able to eat. If natural teeth are rotting and painful or dentures don't fit appropriately, nutrition will suffer. The ability to swallow appropriately is also significant, as individuals who suffer from impaired swallowing (also known as dysphagia) may experience increased discomfort with eating and be at a high risk of choking or developing aspiration pneumonia (in which food particles end up in the lungs instead of the stomach). Dysphagia may result from certain disease processes such as a stroke, Parkinson's, or gastroesophageal reflux disease. Sometimes the cause of dysphagia is unidentifiable; nevertheless, changing the texture of foods as well as the thickness of liquids consumed may be necessary for the individual's safety and nutritional health.

Medical conditions affecting the gastrointestinal tract clearly play a role in diet and nutrition, but so do less obvious medical conditions that affect a person's mobility. Does the individual have the endurance and strength to navigate through a store to purchase groceries? What about carrying the grocery bags into the house once he/she gets home? One solution to these difficulties is home delivery. Check with your local grocery store for details on the service. Mobility also affects the meal preparation process as the design and organization of the kitchen will dictate how much mobility is required. Frequently used items should be kept in cabinets that are within easy reach, and a table to sit and work at is helpful for those who cannot stand for long periods.

Another factor which may affect an individual's desire to eat or cause a change in eating habits is medication. Older adults often take more medications than younger ones, and these medications can have side effects, including loss of appetite or alterations in smell and taste. If a loss of appetite is experienced, check with a physician to determine if a medication could be the cause. Some loss of smell normally occurs with aging, but medications, illness, injury, and smoking can be additional causes. Loss of taste occurs less frequently than loss of smell, and normal aging changes are only slight and usually unnoticeable. However, because the senses of smell and taste are closely linked, one may interpret the loss of smell to instead be that of taste. In turn, the use of increased amounts of salt or sugar to compensate for the loss could be dangerous for people who have high blood pressure or diabetes and should be following special diets. The use of other seasonings, such as lemon juice, vinegar, or herbs, may safely improve the flavors of foods which taste bland. Food safety also becomes a risk when these senses are affected because a person has a decreased ability to detect spoiled food.

The condition of dementia presents its own unique set of complications related to mealtime. Someone in the early stages of dementia may forget or incorrectly measure ingredients when cooking, which will affect the taste of the food and can cause frustration and negative associations with meals. As dementia progresses, individuals may forget to eat, forget that they just ate a regular meal and insist that they are hungry, or forget which meal of the day they are eating (and request certain foods not traditionally served at that time of day). Food preferences may be forgotten, which can lead to disagreements with caregivers and dissatisfaction with food choices, resulting in less than ideal food intake. The ability to independently put together even a simple meal will become unmanageable. During the final stages of dementia, the inability to feed oneself and to chew and swallow food appropriately is present.

While these physical factors influence an older adult's nutritional status, there are also social factors which play important roles in the ability and desire of older adults to prepare and consume meals, which help them maintain adequate nutritional health.

Finances are one social factor which can affect an older adult's nutritional choices. Processed foods, which are often less expensive than fresh foods, pose an issue for older adults with lower income levels and assets. Purchasing processed foods may not be the best health choice if an individual should be following a special diet. The Commonwealth of Pennsylvania provides financial assistance for groceries for those who qualify through the Supplemental Nutrition Assistance Program (formerly known as food stamps). This program is administered by the Department of Human Services, and additional information can be obtained by visiting *www.dhs.state.pa.us*. Information about healthy eating on a low budget and stretching your food dollars is also available on this site. Other local programs include food banks and senior centers. The Cumberland County Aging & Community Services office can provide contact information for these programs. At senior centers, the low-cost hot meals available have the added benefits of socialization and someone else to do the cooking. Local churches may also offer hot meals which are open to the public either on a routine basis or for special occasions.

Another consideration is the older adult's lifelong habits related to meals, including food preferences and mealtime patterns (such as staying at home versus going out to eat, eating alone or with others, and timing of meals). The ability to eat preferred foods may be hampered by some of the factors that we have already discussed, such as oral health and medical conditions. Older adults may feel less inclined to eat if their routines have changed or their days lack other activities to provide structure. If someone is accustomed to dining out on a regular basis, changes in the ability to drive or in the health of dining companions will impact his/her nutritional status. The loss of a spouse can be nutritionally devastating as well for a number of reasons. Perhaps the spouse took primary responsibility for meal planning and preparation, and the surviving individual doesn't enjoy cooking or even know how to cook. Some older adults don't want to take time to cook a full meal for just one person. The loss of companionship during meal time can be an even bigger hurdle to overcome. In a study of 600 older adults who live alone, Home Instead Senior Care found that the majority reported that they eat more nutritiously and that food actually tastes better when they eat with others instead of eating alone, and 85 percent reported that having someone to share their meals with makes mealtimes more satisfying. The same study found that men were twice as likely as women to desire assistance with activities related to meals such as shopping and preparation.

Older adults who live in care facilities or with family members can be regularly monitored for nutritional risks, and support to initiate interventions is readily available when needed. However, identifying older adults at risk for nutritional deficiencies and finding strategies to combat those risks can be more complicated if they live alone in the community. Living alone (and thus probably eating alone) is a significant risk by itself, but it can also amplify some of the other risk factors that we've mentioned. The potential magnitude of this issue is overwhelming to consider, since the US Department of Health and Human Services reported that, as of 2012, 11.8 million older Americans were living alone. The likelihood of living alone also increases as people age (46 percent of women age 75+ live alone, as reported by the Administration on Aging—A Profile of Older Americans 2012).

While being aware of risk factors is an important start to addressing the issue of older adults and nutrition, awareness without action is useless. How can you help? Challenge yourself to find an opportunity to promote healthy nutrition for an older adult who may be at risk. Invite the person to share a meal, take him/her grocery shopping, or assist him/her with some "spring cleaning" in the kitchen (when was the last time the refrigerator received a good review of contents and a scrubbing?). Healthy eating for older adults involves a lot more than just food choices, and the time spent with others may be even more valuable than the food itself.

Karen Kaslow

UNDERSTANDING DEMENTIA

Many people incorrectly use the terms dementia and Alzheimer's disease synonymously. Dementia is an umbrella term that describes a set of symptoms in which thinking, reasoning, and memory are impaired, and these symptoms interfere with an individual's ability to function in daily life. Alzheimer's disease is only one type of dementia.

First, it is important to determine if the signs an individual demonstrates are normal forgetfulness or actually dementia. It is not uncommon, especially as we age, to occasionally misplace items or forget a name or important date. But if an individual begins to ask repetitive questions, has difficulty following directions, puts things in odd places, or demonstrates confusion in familiar places or with familiar tasks (such as paying bills or cooking a meal), it is time to see the doctor.

An evaluation by a physician for symptoms of confusion and forgetfulness might yield some surprising results. For a diagnosis of dementia to be made, impairments must be present in at least two of the following primary mental functions: memory, communication and language, ability to focus and pay attention, reasoning and judgement, and visual perception. There are some conditions which manifest themselves with these symptoms, and when the underlying condition is treated, the confusion and forgetfulness disappear. Some examples of conditions that cause reversible dementias are depression, infections (in the elderly, urinary tract infections are a classic cause), thyroid disease, nutritional deficiencies (especially the B vitamins), low blood sugar, medication side effects or interactions between medications, and substance abuse. There are, however, other causes of dementia which are irreversible. Alzheimer's disease is the most common, but other causes include Lewy body dementia, Pick's disease, Parkinson's disease, frontotemporal disorders, vascular dementia, head injury, and the less common Creutzfeldt-Jakob and Huntington's diseases. While some of these conditions may have no prevention and/or cure, early diagnosis and treatment may slow the progression of symptoms and allow individuals and families time to plan and prepare for the changes that will occur.

The symptoms of dementia which develop will depend upon the area of the brain that is affected. The various underlying disease processes cause damage to brain cells in particular areas, interfering with their function and ability to communicate with each other and leading to cell death. While memory impairment is most often associated with dementia, there are some types of dementia in which personality changes or deficits in executive function (tasks such as decision making or language) are the primary symptoms.

Despite a variety of underlying causes, there are some interventions which may be helpful for anyone experiencing symptoms of dementia. Communication and environment are the key factors for managing the care of an affected individual. A greater likelihood of successful communication occurs when individuals are allowed to live in their own reality. People often want to try to re-orient someone who is confused and believe this approach is appropriate. However, attempts at logical reasoning with individuals who have dementia are futile exercises that only result in frustration on all sides. The Alzheimer's Association website lists additional tips for how others should approach conversation with an individual with dementia as well as how to help the affected individual communicate his/her thoughts. An individual with dementia can be easily overwhelmed, so an awareness of nonverbal cues and body language can help caregivers and families learn when to change course and avoid certain topics of discussion or situations which might trigger additional stress for both parties. An environment with adequate, low-glare lighting, familiar objects, low noise levels, and a structured schedule can contribute to a greater sense of comfort and may promote greater stability in the individual's functioning and behavior.

Watching the progression of dementia is a heart-breaking process. An individual's general state of health and the underlying cause of the dementia determine how slowly or rapidly the dementia symptoms progress. Families may feel they have "lost" their loved one long before the individual dies. Medications may be used to try to slow the progression of symptoms or manage difficult behaviors, but the challenges of maintaining connections to the surrounding world and providing dignity remain.

Alzheimer's Disease

The most common type of dementia is Alzheimer's Disease (AD). This disease was first identified in 1906 when Dr. Alois Alzheimer examined the brain of a woman who had died of a mental illness that had included symptoms of memory loss, language problems, and unpredictable behavior. He noticed changes in the brain tissue that today we call plaques and tangles. Plaques are abnormal clumps of a certain type of protein that are found in the spaces between the brain cells. Tangles occur inside the brain cells when a different type of protein becomes twisted and sticks together. These plaques and tangles ultimately lead to cell death and, as cells die, the affected areas of the brain begin to shrink.

In about 5 percent of all people with AD, the onset of the disease occurs between the ages of 30 and 60 and is referred to as early-onset Alzheimer's. Most cases of early-onset AD result from genetic factors, and scientists are still studying the relationship between certain types of genes and the development of AD.

AD is not a normal part of aging but most commonly occurs in people over age 65; this type of AD is called late-onset. Increasing age is the greatest risk factor for AD and, after age 65, the risk of developing AD doubles every five years.

The Alzheimer's Association has identified ten warning signs of dementia. These include:

- Memory changes that disrupt daily life

- Challenges in planning or solving problems

- Difficulty completing familiar tasks at home, work, or leisure

- Confusion with time or place

- Trouble understanding visual images and spatial relationships

- New problems with words in speaking or writing

- Misplacing items and losing the ability to retrace steps

- Decreased or poor judgment

- Withdrawal from work or social activities

- Changes in mood and personality

For specific examples of these warning signs and how to distinguish them from normal behavior, visit the Alzheimer's Association website.

There is no single test to diagnose AD, but a thorough medical evaluation will help rule out other possible causes of dementia symptoms. Women are more likely to develop AD than men, and life expectancy depends upon an individual's age at diagnosis and general state of health. Younger and healthier individuals may live as long as 20 years. AD is a progressive disease, and individuals eventually move from the early stages of mild forgetfulness to demonstrating increasing levels of cognitive deficiency such as poor concentration, the inability to perform complex tasks, loss of personal memories, and general confusion. Some affected individuals may demonstrate wandering behavior, sleep disturbances, hallucinations (such as seeing or hearing things that aren't really there), delusions (false beliefs such as someone is stealing from them or a spouse is being unfaithful), repetitive behaviors (such as picking at or rubbing something) and/or periods of agitation. Care needs increase gradually as cognition declines, and physical assistance with dressing, eating, and toileting will be required. Eventually, during the latest stages of the disease, physical functioning is affected and difficulties with walking, sitting, swallowing, and general movement occur. During the course of AD, symptoms may be treated with medications and environmental/behavioral interventions. Unfortunately, there is no cure for AD at this time.

Vascular Dementia, Mixed Dementia, and Research

After Alzheimer's Disease, vascular dementia is usually considered the second most common type, comprising about 20 percent of dementia cases. Unlike AD, which progresses slowly, vascular dementia has a sudden onset. Vascular dementia occurs when the blood flow to the brain is compromised, thus depriving the brain of oxygen. This compromise can result from a stroke, in which a clot blocks blood flow, or damage to and breakdown of blood vessel walls due to the build-up of plaque. Either way, damage to nerve cells results in symptoms of dementia. Vascular dementia is more common when multiple strokes affecting both sides of the brain have occurred (multi-infarct dementia), but it can also occur from a single large stroke. Another form of vascular dementia occurs when "hardening of the arteries" causes thickening and narrowing of the small blood vessels found in brain tissue where special cells exist which help nerves communicate with each other. The important factor to remember is that some risk factors for strokes and this type of dementia can be controlled with lifestyle choices and medications, thus lowering your chances of developing either condition. These risk factors include hypertension, diabetes, smoking, atrial fibrillation, and high cholesterol.

As researchers have continued to study dementia, some have found that when looking at autopsy results, in a significant number of cases the neurodegenerative changes of AD and vascular changes coexisted. This condition is known as mixed dementia. Because some of the dementia-related changes in the brain are difficult to determine and study while individuals are alive, people experiencing dementia are often diagnosed with only one type. It is not yet understood how the different types of dementia influence each other or how to determine which symptoms are attributable to which type of dementia when mixed dementia is present. It is possible that mixed dementia is actually the most common type of dementia in the elderly, which has important implications for future research.

Lewy Body Dementia

In addition to AD and vascular dementia, another one of the most common types of dementia is Dementia with Lewy bodies (DLB). Lewy bodies are abnormal, balloon-like structures made up of a certain type of protein. They form inside nerve cells and were first discovered by German neurologist Dr. Friederich Lewy in 1912. Why they form is not yet understood. Dementia with Lewy bodies is related to Parkinson's disease dementia, so both will be discussed in this article.

Dementia with Lewy bodies is often difficult to diagnose

93

because its symptoms can mimic AD and Parkinson's disease when it occurs alone, but it can also co-exist with these two diseases. Symptoms similar to Alzheimer's disease include memory loss, confusion, and poor judgment. Symptoms similar to Parkinson's disease include changes in movement/posture and difficulty with alertness and attention. Sometimes certain symptoms such as difficulty sleeping, loss of smell, and visual hallucinations may occur years before other more classic symptoms develop, leading to a misdiagnosis until the disease enters its later stages. When DLB is present, cognitive symptoms usually appear within one year of symptoms involving movement and postural changes. When Parkinson's disease dementia occurs, the cognitive symptoms usually don't develop until more than one year after the movement changes manifest themselves. While not everyone who is diagnosed with Parkinson's disease will develop dementia, those who are diagnosed with it late in life are more likely to develop Parkinson's disease dementia.

Not everyone with DLB will experience all of its symptoms. In addition to symptoms of altered thinking ability, unpredictable fluctuations in cognitive functioning (concentration, attention, and alertness) can occur, such as staring into space for periods of time or a several-hour nap during the day despite a full night's sleep. Visual hallucinations are common, and auditory hallucinations occasionally occur. Movement symptoms can include changes in handwriting, muscle rigidity or stiffness, a shuffling or awkward gait, tremors (usually in the hands while at rest), stooped posture, trouble with balance or unexplained falls, decreased facial expressions, difficulty swallowing, or a weak voice. Sleep disorders are common, including REM behavior disorder, in which the person seems to act out dreams, has violent movements, or falls out of bed. Mood and behavioral changes may also accompany DLB, and patients may demonstrate extreme sensitivity to antipsychotic medications used to treat these symptoms.

DLB usually begins in people over age 50 and, like Alzheimer's disease, symptoms start slowly and lead to increasing deterioration in cognitive and physical functioning. A brain autopsy after death is the only method of definitively diagnosing this condition, and researchers currently are studying ways to more accurately diagnose it in the living brain. At the present time, there is no cure or method of slowing the progression of DLB. Treatment focuses on controlling the symptoms. A neurologist who specializes in dementia and movement disorders can provide guidance and assistance for those who are affected by the symptoms of Dementia with Lewy bodies.

Frontotemporal Dementia

A less common type of dementia, frontotemporal dementia, accounts for up to 10 percent of all dementia cases. This type of dementia primarily affects two lobes of the brain, the frontal and temporal lobes, hence its name. The degeneration which occurs can result in changes in personality and behavior and/or difficulties with language. This condition usually occurs in individuals in their fifties or early sixties, and, while for some, specific genetic mutations are the cause of the disease, others who are affected have no family history of dementia. There are no other risk factors.

As with all of the other types of dementia that we have discussed, the abnormal behavior of specific proteins in the brain results in damage to nerve cells, which leads to dementia symptoms. Diagnosis is made by observation of symptoms, neurological testing, and testing to rule out other disease processes. There is no cure or method to slow the progression of the disease, and treatment focuses on symptom management.

Frontotemporal dementia can be divided into three main categories based on the primary symptoms that are present. The first category is behavior type. Individuals in this category may experience dramatic personality changes and become socially inappropriate, impulsive, or emotionally indifferent. They demonstrate distractibility, a loss of empathy and tact, a lack of judgment and inhibition, an increased interest in sex, repetitive or compulsive behaviors, a neglect of personal hygiene, and a lack of insight into their own behavior as well as the behavior of others. When apathy is experienced, a misdiagnosis of depression may be made due to decreased energy and motivation. Weight gain may occur due to impulsive eating and decreased activity. When sleep disturbances accompany the behavior type, symptoms may be exacerbated and progress more quickly. These individuals are living in the moment, and in conversation, they may have difficulty transitioning between the past, present, and future.

A second category of frontotemporal dementia is primary progressive aphasia. In the early stages, impairment of language skills is the primary symptom, but behavioral symptoms may develop as the condition progresses. There are two subtypes of primary progressive aphasia: semantic dementia and progressive nonfluent aphasia. In semantic dementia, a person's actual speech is fluent and grammatically correct, but the content of that speech does not relate to the conversation taking place or make sense. Vocabulary becomes increasingly limited, and broad terms may be used in place of more specific ones (for example, "building" instead of "house"). Difficulty understanding spoken and written language may also be present. The second subtype, progressive nonfluent aphasia, manifests itself in language which contains short halting phrases, spelling errors, and incorrect grammar. Individuals have some sense of understanding and remain rational, but they become concrete in their thinking, and their language deficits make answering questions difficult. The ability to read and write may be impaired.

The third category is movement disorders, in which certain automatic muscle functions are affected. Two different subtypes exist, the first exhibiting symptoms of shakiness, lack of coordination, and muscle rigidity/spasms. The second causes balance problems and difficulty walking, frequent falls, and muscle stiffness, especially in the neck and upper body. Slowing and reduced control of eye movements may be another symptom. Frontotemporal dementia used to be known as Pick's disease and is still referred to by that name by some professionals. The progression of the disease is rapid in some, occurring over two to three years, while it may stretch over ten years for others. As with other types of dementia, the physical and emotional toll on affected individuals and their caregivers can be overwhelming. Until a method of prevention or a cure is found, continued research is vital to understanding the risk factors, physical and cognitive effects, and treatment possibilities for all types of dementia.

Karen Kaslow

DISTINGUISHING BETWEEN DEMENTIA AND DELIRIUM

A loved one is experiencing changes in his/her behavior, thinking skills, and/or general emotional state. Family members may initially attribute these changes to the onset of dementia. However, there is a separate and distinct condition, with symptoms similar to dementia, which should be considered in some cases. This condition is called delirium.

The symptoms that one may see with delirium are numerous. One of the classic signs is a lack of focus. An individual's awareness of their environment is reduced and he/she becomes unable to follow a conversation or respond appropriately to questions, easily distracted by unimportant details, or fixated on a certain idea. Sometimes withdrawal occurs, and the individual demonstrates little or no response to environmental stimuli. A lack of focus may be accompanied by changes in behavior such as hallucinations, restlessness or agitation, mixing up days and nights, or frequent verbalizations such as moaning or calling out. The impairment of thinking skills is evidenced by decreased memory (especially short-term); disorientation; speech that is rambling or doesn't make sense; and changes in reading, writing, and understanding language. Emotional symptoms may include anxiety, fear, or paranoia; irritability; euphoria; apathy; or rapid and unpredictable mood swings.

All of the above symptoms may sound like dementia, but

the key difference in delirium is that these symptoms have a rapid onset, usually within several hours or days. With dementia, the symptoms have a gradual and more subtle onset. Symptoms of delirium may also vary widely during the course of a day, and are usually more evident at night as darkness makes the environment even more difficult to interpret. Symptoms of dementia will not fluctuate as much as those of delirium. Dementia and delirium can co-exist, and an underlying dementia may make delirium more difficult to diagnose. Delirium occurs as a result of a stressor on the body. Factors which can contribute to the development of delirium include chronic illness, surgery, infection, certain medications (sleep aids, allergy and pain medications, to name a few), alcohol or drug withdrawal, and metabolic imbalances. Certain individuals are more likely to develop delirium when their bodies experience these stressors. Risk factors include a history of a condition which impacts brain function such as dementia, Parkinson's disease, or stroke; age (older folks are more susceptible); the presence of visual or hearing impairments; depression; and previous episodes of delirium.

How long does delirium last? The overall health of the individual and the ability to address the specific stressor which triggered the delirium will impact whether a delirium will last a few hours or a few weeks or months. Individuals with dementia or other serious, chronic medical conditions may not completely recover from delirium, and may demonstrate a decline in cognition and physical functioning even after the episode of delirium has resolved.

The treatment of delirium will focus on the identification and treatment of the stressor which triggered the symptoms. Other interventions which will aid in the recovery process include measures to create a calm and comfortable environment such as low noise levels, a stable daily routine, consistent caregivers, adequate rest and nutrition, the presence of familiar objects, simple and clear communication, appropriate lighting for the time of day, and pain control.

Delirium, dementia, and depression all have a significant impact on quality of life, and a suspicion of any one of these conditions should be brought to the attention of a health care provider. Since delirium is a reversible condition, distinguishing its symptoms from those of an underlying dementia or depression is important in order for appropriate treatment to be initiated. Family members and friends can provide background information which is essential for a correct diagnosis as well as support to speed the recovery process.

Karen Kaslow

GOVERNMENT BENEFITS

MEDICARE REFRESHER

If you are enrolled in Medicare and believe that there is nothing else to do after your initial enrollment, here are a few important reminders. On the other hand, if you are beginning to think about enrolling in Medicare, this general information can help you get started.

Parts of Medicare

- Part A is hospital insurance. This type of coverage applies to hospital stays, hospice, rehabilitation in a skilled nursing facility, and some home health services (certain conditions apply). Part A is administered by the federal government under Traditional Medicare.

- Part B is medical insurance. Physician services, outpatient care, medical supplies, and preventive services are covered under Part B. Part B is administered by the federal government under Traditional Medicare.

- Part C is a combination of Part A and Part B coverage that is administered by private insurance companies which have contracted with Medicare. These plans are called Medicare Advantage plans.

- Part D is prescription drug coverage. Some Part C plans may already include this coverage, or it may be purchased separately.

Eligibility

- Those who are eligible for Medicare at age 65 have a 7-month initial enrollment period to sign up for the coverage types listed above. This period includes the 3 months prior to one's 65th birthday, the month of the 65th birthday, and the 3 months following the birthday.

- Individuals who have a disability, end-stage renal disease, or who receive Medicaid may have different eligibility dates than their 65th birthdays.

- Some individuals may qualify automatically for Medicare while others may need to sign up. Visit *www.medicare.gov* and use the calculator to determine eligibility or call your local Social Security office.

Costs

- Part A—Usually there is no premium for Part A if you or your spouse worked for at least 10 years (40 calendar quarters) and made payments to Social Security.

- Part B—Most people pay the standard premium amount of $104.90 if they enroll when initially eligible. An extra charge may be added if an individual's modified adjusted gross income on his/her IRS return is above a certain amount. Penalties may apply if an individual doesn't enroll when initially eligible. Deductibles, coinsurance, and copays may also apply.

- Part C—Participants must pay the same monthly premium that applies to those enrolled in Traditional Medicare Part B. Additional costs may include extra monthly premiums, annual deductibles, copayments, and charges for using out-of-network providers. These costs depend on the type of Medicare Advantage plan chosen. These plans may also change their benefits, premiums, and copayments annually.

- Part D—Costs will vary depending on the plan you choose and the types of medication that you take. **These plans should be reviewed annually due to changes in premiums, your prescriptions, and pharmacy formularies** (their list of covered medications).

Important Annual Dates

- January 1—March 31: This is a general enrollment period for those who did not enroll in Medicare when they were initially eligible.

- January 1—February 14: Individuals may choose to change from a Medicare Advantage plan (Part C) to Traditional Medicare (Parts A and B) and a drug plan (Part D).

- October 15—December 7: Open enrollment period during which one may change from Traditional Medicare to a Medicare Advantage plan; change from a Medicare Advantage plan to

Traditional Medicare; change from one Medicare Advantage plan to another; or join, drop, or change a Medicare drug plan.

Choosing Medicare coverage may sound like a daunting task. While there are many details to consider, the government website *www.medicare.gov* contains information written in plain English and organized by specific topics. Taking the time to understand the various Medicare benefits which are available may save you money and surprises later on when specific types of benefits are needed.

Karen Kaslow

TRADITIONAL (ORIGINAL) MEDICARE V. MEDICARE ADVANTAGE PLANS

It can be a challenge to determine if traditional Medicare or a Medicare Advantage plan will provide "the best" coverage for a particular individual. Traditional Medicare is administered by the federal government, and Medicare Advantage plans are administered by private insurance companies. An important difference between Traditional Medicare and an Advantage plan involves access to services. With Traditional Medicare, an individual may visit any health care provider that accepts Medicare anywhere in the U.S. for either routine or emergency care. Referrals and pre-authorization for services are NOT required. It is important to note that some physicians and other types of providers are not enrolled in Medicare. Medicare Advantage programs have a more structured approach to routine care, which often involves a specific primary care physician as a gatekeeper for a network of specialists and other providers. Referrals and pre-authorization of services may be required.

Older adults who have chronic disease conditions which periodically require hospitalization and an extended period of care afterward should take note of the following observation. Within our practice of elder law and life care planning, our staff has encountered differences in the way Traditional Medicare and Medicare Advantage plans manage the reimbursement of rehabilitation services provided in nursing homes. Following a hospitalization, older adults who require ongoing care in addition to therapy may be referred to a skilled nursing facility for these services. Traditional Medicare will pay in full for the first 20 days of this type of care, and then a copay is required for the remainder of the stay, which may potentially be up to a total of 100 days, depending on the individual's diagnosis and response to therapy and nursing services. The nursing facilities determine when Medicare coverage should end according to Medicare guidelines and based on their direct observations.

With Medicare Advantage plans, private insurance companies keep tighter reins on their expenses. They often only approve a certain number of days of coverage at a time, and then the nursing facility must provide a status update before the insurance company will approve or deny continuation of benefits. Due to this more intense regulation of care, individuals with Medicare Advantage plans may not receive as many days of coverage as those with a similar diagnosis who have Traditional Medicare.

Both types of Medicare programs have an appeal process for unfavorable coverage determinations. The first appeal must be made by telephone within 48 hours of receiving the denial notice; however, Medicare appeals rarely succeed at this initial level. Legal assistance is not required to file an appeal and Medicare will not reimburse legal fees related to an appeal, even if the initial coverage determination was incorrect. A difficult choice must be made between ending rehabilitation services for which Medicare coverage has been denied or paying privately.

The Center for Medicare Advocacy website (*www.medicareadvocacy.org*) contains additional information and provides guidelines for how to research and choose between Traditional Medicare and Medicare Advantage plans. The less expensive option offered by a former employer's retirement program might not be the best choice. Medicare Advantage participants should confirm not only which doctors and hospitals will be available under a particular plan but also which nursing homes may be used for rehabilitation.

Dave Nesbit, Karen Kaslow

THE INS AND OUTS OF MEDIGAP POLICIES

When choosing between Traditional Medicare and Medicare Advantage plans, the option for a supplemental plan should also factor into your decision. These supplemental plans are called Medigap policies, and they are sold by private insurance companies. Medigap policies help cover some of the out-of-pocket expenses that Medicare doesn't pay for, such as deductibles, copayments, and health care provided outside of the United States. There are some general guidelines to remember when thinking about Medigap policies.

- Medigap policies are only available to individuals who are enrolled in Original Medicare. If you have a Medicare Advantage plan, you cannot enroll in a Medigap plan unless you disenroll from the Medicare Advantage plan and return to Original Medicare. In addition, you must have both Part A and Part B coverage to obtain a Medigap plan.

- You must pay a monthly premium for a Medigap policy that is separate from your monthly Part B premium for Medicare.

- Medigap policies only cover one person. Spouses must each purchase a separate policy if they both desire coverage.

- Medigap policies sold after January 1, 2006 are not allowed to include prescription drug coverage.

Purchase of a Part D plan is needed to cover your medications.

- Multiple companies can sell Medigap policies within any state, but the plans themselves are standardized according to state and federal regulations and are usually identified by letter (for example Plan K will offer the same benefits no matter what company is selling it, but the premiums may vary among companies).

- As long as you pay your premium, your insurance company cannot cancel your Medigap policy, even if you develop health problems.

- Medigap policies usually do NOT cover expenses such as hearing aids, vision care and glasses, long term care, dental care, or private duty nursing.

Perhaps the most important factor to be aware of when choosing your Medigap policy is the fact that if you enroll in a Medigap plan during the first six months of eligibility for Medicare, you can purchase ANY POLICY from ANY COMPANY regardless of your health, and pay the SAME COST as a healthy person. After those six months, insurance companies will use medical underwriting to determine whether or not to accept your application and how much to charge you. There are a few special situations that may allow individuals with certain health conditions to change to Medigap plans after their initial enrollment periods. See *www.medicare.gov* for details about these situations, plans available in your state, and additional information about Medigap insurance. For most folks seeking a Medigap policy, do your homework and *choose wisely the first time to prevent a more complicated and expensive process later on.*

Karen Kaslow

WHAT MEDICARE PAYS FOR IN A SKILLED NURSING FACILITY

Since Title 18 of the Social Security Act Amendments of 1965 introduced Medicare, American citizens have confidently expected that, when we reach age 65, Medicare will be available to pay for health care. Permanent resident aliens may also qualify for Medicare at age 65 if they have lived in the United States continuously for at least 5 years and pay the Medicare Part A premium. Persons who are permanently disabled, have ALS, or have an end-stage renal condition can qualify at a younger age.

Many persons are surprised that, as a general rule, Medicare does not pay for long-term care in a skilled nursing facility. To get Medicare to pay for any care in a skilled nursing facility, it is necessary that a patient be admitted within 30 days of admission to a hospital for at least 3 consecutive days. A day is usually counted if a patient is present at midnight.

A physician must certify that the patient's care is not only needed but, as a practical matter, that the care is only available in a skilled nursing facility on an inpatient basis. The skilled nursing facility must be approved by the Centers for Medicare & Medicaid Services (CMS). Medicare will pay for care in a skilled nursing facility for up to 100 days, after which a patient is expected to pay privately until his/her financial resources have been depleted to the point that he/she becomes eligible for Medicaid.

Some people are surprised that The Affordable Care Act (a.k.a. the ACA or "Obamacare") did not extend the payment for care in a skilled nursing home. The principal element of the ACA related to the cost of long-term care was the Community Living Assistance Services and Support Program (a.k.a. the CLASS Act). However, the CLASS Act was determined to be actuarially unsound, abandoned by the Obama administration in October 2011, and repealed by Fiscal Cliff legislation in January 2013.

The federal regulations pertaining to who pays for what and when in a skilled nursing home are confusing even to most lawyers. Families get angry at hospitals when they learn that Medicare will not pay for skilled nursing because the time the patient spent in the hospital was an "observation" stay and not an "admission" or the length of admission was less than three days. Families also get upset when a skilled nursing facility says that Medicare has ended and that the patient must pay with personal funds.

Since authorization by the Medicare Modernization Act of 2003, Medicare charges by health care providers are monitored by Recovery Audit Contractors (RACs), who are agents of CMS. Because RACs are paid contingent fees for the overpayments that they detect and recover, the health care providers are highly motivated to enforce the Medicare rules strictly. It is fair to say that society shares responsibility for an imperfect system that gives both hospitals and skilled nursing facilities the unpleasant task of denying Medicare and demanding private payments.

The Medicare rules demand that a patient must require the type of rehabilitation services offered by the skilled nursing facility for five days per week or skilled nursing services offered seven days per week. Therefore, a patient would not qualify for skilled nursing if a need for wound care or physical therapy could be met by a visit every other day to his/her home by a nurse. Some specific services, such as tube feedings, require admission to a skilled nursing facility.

Assuming a patient qualifies for Medicare in a skilled nursing facility, full coverage of expenses is provided for the first 20 days. From days 21 through 100, a daily copayment is required. Medicare supplemental insurance can pay for this if the patient was able to afford that insurance and was wise enough to choose it as an option. Until recently, the CMS had required care providers to declare that "improvement" was occurring or Medicare would be terminated. Persons who were evaluated to be stable, chronic, or in need of maintenance only were told that their eligibility for Medicare had ended. Often, this would happen long before 100 days had elapsed.

A federal court case decided in January 2013, *Jimmo v Sebelius*, changed that. The judge in that case approved a settlement between the nursing home patient and the federal Medicare system, which was represented by Health and Human Services Secretary Kathleen Sebelius. The impact of the settlement created a new federal policy related to Medicare eligibility in skilled nursing facilities. No longer must a patient show improvement in order to have the cost of care in a skilled nursing facility be paid by Medicare. The new standard is that a patient's need for *skilled* care to maintain or slow deterioration of the patient's condition is enough to justify Medicare for the 100 day period. This ruling makes it easier to plan for the time when Medicare ends.

If a skilled nursing facility believes that the patient no longer qualifies for Medicare, a "Notice of Medicare Provider Non-Coverage" must be issued to the patient at least 2 days before the date that the Medicare coverage will end. The patient has the right to appeal this notice by contacting the Quality Improvement Organization (QIO) by no later than noon of the calendar day following receipt of the notice. Directions of how to contact the QIO are on the notice, and the QIO is expected to make a decision within 72 hours.

The details of Medicare rules are confusing. The fact that "Medicare won't pay" does not mean that Medicare

113

supplemental insurance will not. Sometimes caregivers overlook the opportunity to submit claims to their supplemental insurer because of emotional stress and time pressures. Medicare is complicated; when your loved one is in a skilled nursing facility, ask for help. The business office can answer your basic questions and refer you for help when they can't.

Dave Nesbit

PAYING FOR HEALTH CARE WITH MEDICARE AND MEDICAL ASSISTANCE

When people call our office looking for information about long-term care options, we often find that there is a lack of understanding about the differences between Medicare, Medicaid, and Medical Assistance. Karen Scott, the former Director of Admissions at Manor Care Health Services in Carlisle, recently shared that some of the families she works with are shocked to find out that Medicare does not automatically pay for all of nursing home care for extended periods of time. Since the names Medicare and Medicaid sound alike, it is easy to confuse the two. As older adults' health care needs change, planning to pay for the health care can become more complicated if families lack a general understanding of these federal programs.

Medicare is the federal health insurance program that is available for people age 65 and older, people who are under age 65 with certain disabilities, and people of any age who have End Stage Renal Disease. This program is supported by premiums and payroll taxes. As we have clarified, there are four parts to the Medicare program. Let's review:

- **Part A** (Hospital Insurance) - This part covers inpatient hospital stays, *temporary* stays in a nursing home to receive rehabilitation or skilled care, hospice care, and home health care. In order for Medicare to pay for rehabilitation in a nursing

115

home, **an individual must have been admitted to the hospital for at least three nights within the 30 days prior to the nursing home stay.** A distinction is made between individuals who are "admitted" versus "held for observation," so make sure the patient's status is clarified when in the hospital. If the three night admission qualification is met, be aware that Medicare will fully cover the first *twenty days* of a nursing home stay in a Medicare-approved facility. After that, there will be a daily copay charged to the patient for days 21—100. Also note that **100 days is not guaranteed**; the number of days which Medicare will pay for depends on the patient's condition. In our experience, patients with a traditional Medicare plan through the federal government have a greater chance of receiving more covered days than those with a Medicare plan administered by a private insurance company (see Part C below).

- **Part B** (Medical Insurance)—This part covers doctor appointments, medical equipment (such as a walker), outpatient services (such as therapy), some preventive services, and home health care. Premiums for this coverage are deducted from an individual's Social Security or Railroad Retirement benefit. To qualify for home health care under Parts A & B benefits, an individual must require intermittent, *skilled* care from a nurse or therapist, which is ordered by a physician. In addition, the patient must be considered homebound (determined by the physician), and the services must be provided by a Medicare certified agency. Routine personal care and homemaking services are usually not included unless someone is also receiving temporary skilled services.

- **Part C** (Medicare Advantage Plans)—This part combines both Part A and Part B coverage and is administered by Medicare approved private insurance companies. Some plans will also include Part D coverage (see below). Extra benefits and services may be available as part of the plan or for an additional cost.

- **Part D**—This part covers the cost of prescription drugs and is run by private insurance companies.

Medicaid is a combined federal and state program which provides health coverage for people who meet strict income and asset guidelines. Every state has different rules related to Medicaid eligibility. In Pennsylvania, the Medicaid program is called *Medical Assistance*, so these two terms are used interchangeably here. The Pennsylvania Department of Human Services administers this program. Coverage is provided for costs related to hospitalization, nursing home care, doctor visits, medical equipment, home health care, and sometimes medications. While Medical Assistance is often thought of as coverage for those who are low-income, this benefit can also be used by middle class families to supplement income to pay for long-term care in a nursing home. There are strict regulations which must be met to qualify for Medical Assistance, and unless one has limited income and assets, the aid of an elder law attorney may be required during the application process. It is important to note that neither Medicare nor Medicaid cover the cost of care in a Personal Care Home or Assisted Living Facility.

As you can see, Medicare and Medicaid are two different programs with varied eligibility requirements and types of benefits. An understanding of these differences can help prevent unwelcome surprises during a health care crisis and lead to improved planning strategies for potential future needs.

Karen Kaslow

SHARING FAMILY RESOURCES WITHOUT PENALTY

Ideally, families provide care out of love. Compensation is a secondary concern, offered graciously as a token of appreciation. However, for many families during economically challenging times, the lines between the ownership of resources of parents and their children become blurred.

If you enjoyed the television series which chronicled the Walton family during the Depression, you remember the love of that intergenerational family as the members supported one another. I can't remember any episode about legal paperwork to justify tuition support paid by Grandpa to help John-Boy get his college education. But neither can I recall an episode about Alzheimer's disease nor the Waltons' need for government help to pay for skilled nursing care.

Family members are often geographically scattered now, more so than during the Depression, and unable to help with home care. People live longer. Government programs have been created to pay for nursing care services. Times have changed since the Walton family's era.

Today, tokens of gratitude, or gifts of love, are problems with the government when applying for financial assistance for nursing care. Paying the tuition of a grandchild or putting an adult child's name on a house deed or bank account might be intended as a fair and just reward. However, if the reasoning which justifies the fairness of that gratuitous action is not appropriately documented at the time of the exchange, such a gesture can result in severe hardship for the family. It's at best very risky, if not absolutely too late, to attempt retrospectively at the time of the application for assistance to document and justify a previous gratuitous action.

It would never occur to most people to have a written agreement in place to document the activities of family members to care for a loved one at home. As long as family caregiving remains a private matter for the rest of the older person's life, it is unlikely that the government will have any occasion to be concerned about token gifts or unreported payments among family members for caregiving. However, it is unwise to discount future possibilities. Home care can sometimes become impossible, such as after a debilitating stroke or the progression of Alzheimer's disease.

When care of an aging parent can no longer be provided safely in the family home, a skilled nursing facility is often the best option. Complex regulations to qualify for government assistance for care in a nursing home have been established to prevent families from scamming the government. Since the average cost of nursing home care in Pennsylvania is more than $100,000 per year, the stakes are high to avoid being disqualified or penalized from receiving medical assistance.

If a person gave away money or property totaling more than $500 in any single month within the sixty months preceding an application to obtain assistance from the Commonwealth to pay for nursing care, it is considered to be "gifting". Gifting is not a crime, but financial assistance for nursing care will not be provided until after a penalty time is imposed. Because the gifting determination is not made by the Commonwealth until after a proper application has been filed and an application will not be considered fully until the applicant's resources have been exhausted, a financial crisis occurs if a determination of "gifting" occurs upon review of the application and a penalty period is assessed before assistance will be provided.

As a practical matter, the family for whom a penalty period has been assessed has to find a way either to recover the gifted money, or somehow otherwise pay for nursing care until the penalty is over. Recent Pennsylvania court actions have referenced the long-overlooked "filial responsibility" laws to require family members to pay nursing home costs for a parent who lacked money to do so and was ineligible for government assistance because of gifting.

Consider the adult child who volunteers to reduce her hours of compensated employment outside the home in order to be available to help her parent. For some families, this makes it impossible to pay for household expenses unless the parent helps the caregiver financially to make up for lost wages. Often, families agree among themselves that it seems acceptable for the parent to pay some of the caregiver's bills, whether it is tuition for a grandchild, a mortgage, or other expenses that might total more than $500 per month.

What seems fair and reasonable within a family creates problems when applying for medical assistance. Financial transfers from a parent to a child generally are considered to be a penalty-triggering gift unless they are reported as wages to the IRS. Under-the-table payment of wages to a caregiver to avoid taxes can lead to a penalty even if paid in cash, since significant cash withdrawals from a parent's accounts need to be accounted for when applying for assistance.

This problem can be avoided by using a family caregiver agreement, and substantial wealth of a parent, including the family home, can be transferred to a child legitimately. The caregiver agreement should be based on a written care plan prepared by a qualified professional. The caregiver agreement references the care plan and details which services the caregiver is providing, the hours "worked" as a caregiver, and the compensation to be paid.

Compensation for caregiving services must reflect the value of the services. The U. S. Bureau of Labor Statistics wage rates show an average of $10 per hour wage for a personal care aide to assist with housekeeping, laundry, errands, and meal preparation. Private agencies charge twice that to provide and supervise such a caregiving employee. A family caregiver compensation rate for non-medical caregiving in the range of $10 to $20 per hour can therefore be justified. A Registered Nurse, whose ordinary market value in wages might be twice that of a personal care aide, may only justify the higher wage as a family caregiver if he or she is actually providing nursing services in relation to a care plan.

It would be helpful if families could see into the future and know whether or not government assistance will be required. Without this ability, families who are sharing resources are wise to seek counsel and educate themselves about the potential pitfalls of private arrangements. Keystone Elder Law P.C.'s specialized knowledge can help you sort out the details and put a plan in place to benefit the entire family. Family caregiving CAN be accomplished without creating financial risk down the road.

Dave Nesbit

VETERANS' BENEFIT FOR LONG-TERM CARE

Do you know the history of Veterans Day, which is celebrated on November 11th? Originally known as "Armistice Day," it was celebrated in 1919 to mark the first anniversary of the cessation of hostilities during WWI (although the Treaty of Versailles, which officially ended the war, was not signed until June 26, 1919). November 11th was designated as a legal holiday in 1938, and, at that time, the focus remained a commemoration of those who served in WWI. In 1954, after experiencing WWII and the Korean War, the government amended the act of 1938 and changed the word "armistice" to "veterans" so that the service of all wartime veterans could be honored. Many wartime veterans who do not have a war-related disability are unaware that, as they become older and possibly require assistance with the functions of daily living, the Veterans Administration (VA) offers a benefit to help pay for this type of care for veterans and/or their spouses if certain qualifications are met.

This benefit is only one type of veterans' pension benefits and is called "Aid and Attendance." To be eligible, the veteran must have served at least one day during a period of war (the dates of wartime are designated by Congress) with a total of 90 days or more of active duty. In addition, the veteran or his/her spouse must meet one of the following conditions:

- Requiring the help of another person to perform daily activities such as bathing, dressing, toileting, feeding, mobility, and continence

- Being primarily bedridden due to a disability

- Residing in a nursing home due to mental or physical incapacity

- Having limited eyesight (corrected to a 5/200 visual acuity or less in both eyes) or concentric contraction of the visual field to 5 degrees or less.

Additional requirements include income and asset considerations. Unlike the federal Medicaid program, which provides specific dollar amounts to define eligibility, the VA instead uses a formula which takes into account numerous factors to calculate eligibility. This formula combines income amounts and net worth as well as factors such as medical expenses, life expectancy, and number of dependents. A general guideline for a married veteran and spouse (as of July, 2016), is that their assets should be less than $80,000 (not including a home or vehicle) in order to be financially eligible for this benefit. Veterans with assets of a greater amount than this would be wise to consult an elder law attorney to determine if there are possible strategies for becoming eligible for this benefit without jeopardizing the possibility of obtaining a different public benefit in the future, since every benefit program has its own unique regulations and requirements.

The VA's current rules allow Veterans who have more than $80,000 to give away their excess assets or convert assets into income (proposed changes to these rules are being considered by Congress at the time of publication of this book). However, the gifting of assets violates the rules of the Medicaid program, which offers more financial help than the VA, and can be necessary to pay for care in a Skilled Nursing Facility. Because an unexpected stroke or orthopedic injury can require permanent relocation to a Skilled Nursing Facility, it is best to get help from an elder law attorney to consider Medicaid rules before making any gift or annuity purchase to qualify for the VA benefits. Despite warnings from the American Association of Retired Persons (AARP) and others, bad advice is still given to veterans who want to qualify immediately for this special pension. There are two common mistakes that veterans make.

Some veterans give their assets to their adult children, assuming that they will be able to get them back if they are needed. But if the veteran's child gets divorced, becomes bankrupt, is sued, injured, or gets into an unexpected situation which causes the assets to be encumbered, other family members can become liable for the future cost of the veteran's care. There are too many unforeseeable issues to use the word never, as in "my child(ren) would 'never' allow my assets to be lost or encumbered."

A second mistake, which is encouraged by annuity salespersons, is to convert excess assets into allowable income through the use of an annuity. The VA is tolerant of annuities and has few restrictions. Unfortunately, most annuities which are acceptable to the VA can cause a vet to be ineligible for Medicaid. Financial consequences are expensive.

Confusion and frustration can occur because the regulations between the VA programs and the Medicaid program are different. Senate Bill 3270 was introduced in 2012 to add restrictions to the VA requirements. However, even if adopted, that legislation would not resolve all the confusion and contradictions between the VA pension and Medicaid.

For additional information about categories of benefits, eligibility requirements, compensation amounts, and the differences between VA pension and Medicaid, visit the US Department of Veterans Affairs website at *www.va.gov*. Information is also available from county Veterans Affairs offices. You may visit any Veterans Affairs office; it does not have to be the one in the county in which the veteran resides.

Dave Nesbit, Karen Kaslow

COMMON MISCONCEPTIONS REGARDING VA LONG TERM CARE

Myth #1—I do not qualify for long term care from a VA facility because I was a Reservist or a member of the National Guard.

Fact: Members of the National Guard and Reserves may be eligible for long term care from the VA if they were called to active duty on a Federal Executive Order and the veteran completed the full call-up period. If you or a loved one served in the National Guard or Reserves, you may qualify for important veterans' benefits to assist with your long term care needs.

Myth #2—I do not qualify for long term care from a VA facility because I do not have a service-connected disability.

Fact: Any veteran who served in the military, even during peacetime, and was honorably discharged may receive long term care provided by the United States Department of Veterans Affairs ("VA"). Generally, priority is given to those veterans who:

- Need nursing care due to a service-connected disability;

- Have a combined disability rating of 70% or more; or

- Have a disability rating of at least 60% and are:

  ✓ Deemed unemployable; or
  ✓ Have been rated permanently and totally disabled.

However, even if a veteran does not meet one of the above requirements, he or she is still eligible to receive long term care from the VA. Services will be provided only if resources are available after the needs of those priority veterans have been met. For further information regarding how the VA prioritizes veterans, please see *www.va.gov/healthbenefits/resources/priority_groups.asp.*

If space is available at a VA or affiliated facility, veterans will be considered on a case by case basis based upon their priority grouping. Therefore, if you or a loved one are a veteran with long term care needs and were honorably discharged from military service, I urge you to contact your county Veterans' Affairs Office to initiate the application process and determine your priority group.

Myth #3 - The closest VA facility is too far from my residence. I want to reside at a closer facility so I cannot receive long term care from a VA facility.

Fact: Many veterans may not even attempt to apply for long term care through the VA because the closest VA facility is too far from family and friends. What they may not be aware of is that veterans can receive the same long term care benefits they would have received in a VA facility at a non-VA facility. In addition to VA owned and operated facilities, the VA provides long term care services to veterans through two other programs: 1) State Veterans' Homes owned and operated by each participating state; and 2) the community nursing home program. Most veterans are unaware that there are some private nursing homes in their community that contract with the VA to designate a certain number of beds to be available for veterans who need care. In Cumberland County, one such facility is Claremont Nursing and Rehabilitation Center in Carlisle. However, stays in such contracted facilities may be limited for veterans with a disability rating lower than 70% and for veterans who do not need care due to a service-connected disability. To determine whether you or a loved one may qualify to receive long term care at a community nursing home, you should contact a trusted VA accredited elder law attorney who can assist you with your questions.

Myth #4—I do not qualify for long term care from a VA facility because I am a surviving spouse of a veteran.

Fact: There are over 9 million surviving spouses of veterans currently living in the United States. Many of these spouses are receiving long term care or will need it in the future. However, many have no idea that they may be eligible to receive long term care in a VA or affiliated facility as a surviving spouse of a veteran. Federal regulations permit up to 25% of the beds of a State Veteran home to be designated for veteran-related family members (i.e. spouse, surviving spouse, and/or Gold Star parents). Surviving spouses of veterans may also qualify for the Aid and Attendance benefit, a little known pension benefit that can be utilized to pay for long term care costs. To receive the benefit, the veteran must have served at least ninety (90) days of active duty, with at least one of those days occurring during a wartime period. The spouse must need assistance with at least two (2) activities of daily living (e.g. bathing, feeding, dressing, mobility, etc.). If you or your loved one is a surviving spouse of a veteran and are in need of long term care, you may be eligible to receive long term care services in a VA or affiliated facility.

Myth #5—I do not qualify for long term care from a VA facility because I do not need 24 hour skilled nursing care.

Fact: While many veterans receiving long term care provided by the VA or an affiliate are receiving 24 hour skilled nursing care, this is not a requirement for entry into a VA or affiliated facility. Just as a skilled nursing facility may provide additional services such as rehabilitation services and respite care, veterans needing restorative care, mental health recovery care, respite care, and palliative and hospice care also may receive this type of care at a VA or affiliated facility.

Ryan Webber

LEGAL & FINANCIAL PLANNING

THE BASICS OF DESIGNING AND FUNDING AN EXTENDED CARE PLAN

Keystone Elder Law P.C. has evolved to become an "extended care planning and coordination firm." Our expansion of services complements the traditional skills of lawyers and provides a valuable and more comprehensive approach to issues of aging and older persons. The term "extended care" is not used as commonly as the term "long-term care".

"Extended care" more accurately describes what happens when Medicare stops paying for care in a skilled nursing facility after 100 days, yet care is still needed for an undetermined extended period of time. Those who have inherited healthy genes and follow disciplined diet and exercise patterns probably have an increased chance of living a long life. But as they age gracefully, even they eventually could become frail and need an extension of home care services beyond housecleaning and lawn care in order to remain safely at home during their final years. Medicare generally does not pay for regular and ongoing home care assistance with Activities of Daily Living (ADLs).

The initial step of any extended care plan is to make sure that appropriate "foundational legal documents" are in place. Planning should consider the use of an irrevocable trust, which can be a helpful tool in some, but not all, cases. Foundational legal documents, which are important for all clients, include a durable financial power of attorney, a health care power of attorney, an advanced care directive, and a last will and testament. These documents define the preferences of how an individual will surrender control and responsibility to a trusted other person(s) to act legally either on behalf of, or in support of, one's wishes.

The documents can and probably should include different provisions for a married couple that is ten years into retirement and expecting to need extended care than those for a younger married couple. For example, the gifting powers under a durable financial power of attorney for a person on the threshold of needing extended care are broader than would be necessary or advisable for the documents of newlyweds. Also, if one spouse enters a skilled nursing home, it is advisable for the well spouse to alter his/her will to manage the minimum inheritance required from the estate of the ill spouse so that the most beneficial outcome for the family can be obtained.

Ideally, the funding of an extended care plan should be addressed when the basic legal documents are being prepared or updated. Anticipating the probable need for extended care can, on one level, be a function of statistical probability. For example, insurance data suggest that more than 40 percent of persons who reach age 65 will ultimately need some level of extended care, and the typical time that such a claim is made is at age 81. But it is also important to consider the particular health issues which either family genetic history or early-onset medical conditions suggest are likely to be present in the future of the principal clients.

A care plan should consider the lifestyles of both the principals and the extended family. Even if potential family caregivers are available and willing, the impact of the principals' need for regular homecare over an extended period must be evaluated realistically in order to avoid caregiver burnout. Similar consideration should be given to accommodate a desire of the well spouse to continue in an accustomed lifestyle without sacrificing significant personal time or monthly income towards caregiving. The principals should determine if it will be acceptable to erode a planned legacy gift to children, grandchildren, or charity by the depletion of assets in order to pay for care.

Although extremely wealthy persons can afford to self-insure even if it is unwise to do so, middle class couples should confront the economic reality of extended care sooner than later. Suppose a married couple has a history of Alzheimer's disease in the family and wants to make sure that a secure facility can be afforded without sacrificing cash flow for the well spouse or the intended legacy gifts. If both spouses are insurable at age 55, a $2,115 annual investment will produce as much as $687,000 in long-term care insurance benefits by age 81. This reflects an insurance payment of $150 per day increased annually at a compounded rate of 3 percent, which should be enough to pay for secure dementia care. This same insurance would cost a 65-year-old couple $3,250 per year IF their health enabled them to qualify. The value of the insurance would be more than 8 times the compounded value of their investment from self-insuring.

There is no one-size-fits-all for insurance or extended care plans, which should take one's lifestyle, projected monthly income, and other factors into account. Wartime veterans could be eligible to receive a special pension for extended care of nearly $70 per day, so while that is not enough to replace the need for insurance in all cases, as a general rule, a wartime veteran needs less long-term care insurance than a non-veteran. This is especially true if the veteran has optimized his/her ability to receive the pension through the use of trust planning.

Persons whose health excludes them from obtaining insurance should explore a family caregiver agreement or life estate arrangement in tandem or individually. Reverse mortgages can be a good way to pay for home care but should never be used to buy an annuity or other investment.

Sometimes a married couple fails to plan and suffers an

unexpected crisis which begins in an ambulance and ends, after a short stay at a hospital, in a skilled nursing facility. Current laws allow elder law attorneys to juggle assets to accelerate eligibility for public benefits to fund a nursing care solution during a financial crisis. Because law changes are likely to restrict these opportunities in the future, making plans to fund an extended care plan today is important for middle class baby boomers who do not wish to compromise their lifestyles or depend on their children.

Dave Nesbit

COMMON MISTAKES RELATED TO LONG-TERM CARE

Securing long-term care for a loved one can be a complicated process which involves legal, financial, and social factors in addition to physical care needs. Below are some easy-to-make mistakes that can have undesirable consequences for the individual receiving care as well as for the family.

- Powers-of-attorney: It's a big mistake if an individual fails to execute these documents. Especially regarding legal and financial matters, huge headaches can result if a person becomes incapable of handling his/her own affairs and he/she has accounts, property, and other assets only in his/her own name. It can also be a mistake to cut corners with do-it-yourself legal documents. Having a legal piece of paper might be better than nothing, but using it inappropriately could create a new set of problems.

- Have you been designated as a Financial Power-of-Attorney Agent? When signing anything on behalf of another individual, always sign your own name followed by "P.O.A." If you sign your own name as a responsible party to a contract without the "P.O.A.," you could be on the hook financially.

- Is a loved one receiving VA benefits? For certain benefits, an individual's assets are taken into consideration during the application process. An application can take months or sometimes even a year plus to receive approval. If the veteran or surviving spouse owns a house at the time of application and the family needs to sell the house while the VA applicant is living, the proceeds of the sale will cause the VA benefit to be terminated. Consult an attorney before planning to sell a home or property.

- Does your loved one need rehabilitation after a hospitalization? Realize that admission to a hospital for a minimum of three nights is key to getting Medicare to pay for rehabilitation in a nursing home for a minimum of 20 and a maximum of 100 days. Carefully consider his/her potential ability to safely return home after the rehabilitation. Some short-term rehab facilities are not set up to accept Medical Assistance when Medicare stops, and this can be a real problem if your loved one cannot be safely discharged to return home. The adjustment to staying in a nursing home long-term will be much easier if the individual is able to stay in the same facility after the rehabilitation period has ended. Keep in mind the possibility of whether or not Medical Assistance could be available to pay for long-term care services when choosing a rehab facility.

- The nursing home application process: A standard question on nursing home applications is whether or not the potential resident has given financial gifts in the five years prior to admission to the facility. Many applicants may check "No" without an understanding of what constitutes a gift. This answer can create financial complications if the individual eventually runs out of funds and applies for Medical Assistance. A gift is any asset that is given away or transferred for less than fair market value. Specifically, a single gift or the sum of multiple gifts which totals more than $500 in a single month is important to disclose. Examples of gifts are checks written at the holidays, college tuition paid on behalf of a grandchild, household expenses paid for a residence that isn't one's own (including if a parent is living in a child's home so that the child can provide care), and a car given away or sold for less than market value. When these gifts are disclosed during the application process, planning can be done to avoid financial liability later on.

- Personal Liability: If a nursing home tells you, the adult child, that it will do the Medical Assistance application for you and that you don't need a lawyer's help, ask if it will promise not to make a claim against you personally if your parent's application is denied.

These are only a few situations in which uninformed families can find themselves in trouble even when they have the best of intentions. When in doubt, consult an attorney who has knowledge of all of the issues that older adults may face, since rules can vary or overlap in a variety of ways, and the future is always uncertain.

Dave Nesbit, Karen Kaslow

YOU MIGHT BE FINANCIALLY LIABLE FOR YOUR PARENT'S CARE

This article is directed primarily to the attention of the successful, out-of-state adult child who is visiting parents who live in Pennsylvania. Your time and ability to visit throughout much of the year is probably limited. Maybe you are fortunate to have a local sibling who helps your parents with caregiving and finances.

Sometimes, a visitor sees things that are not as apparent to those who are involved in a regular daily routine. It is important to be restrained and diplomatic about your observations. Your local siblings may perceive your well-intended suggestions to be unfair criticism and assignments.

Maybe a curiosity about your parents' finances seems to be unnecessary or inappropriate. But there is a reason for you to be concerned about your parents' finances, especially if dementia is evident and another sibling may have access to family resources while helping with care. Even honest mistakes about how resources are shared between your parents and a needy sibling can create expensive problems for you personally.

Pennsylvania law makes adult children responsible for payment to a nursing home for the care of an indigent parent, unless the parent abandoned the child when the child was a minor for a period of ten years. This area of law is known as filial responsibility. Pennsylvania's law is different and tougher than most states.

In three different cases, the Pennsylvania Superior Court has applied the law to enforce payment by a child for the support of a parent. In one case, a mother brought the action against her son. In two other cases, a collection action was brought against a child by a nursing home, most recently in the Pittas case, when one son was found liable for his mother's $93,000 nursing home bill.

Several topics discussed within the court opinions lead to a few conclusions. Fraudulent action by an adult child is not necessary for liability to be found. No contractual obligation by the adult child is necessary to create liability. A creditor has no duty to bring a collection action against more than one child, who would be forced to bring the other siblings into the case to share the burden.

The definition of indigent is not specific, but certainly a person whose assets have been exhausted by the ongoing expenses of a long-term care facility would be indigent. It shocks many people to discover that payment for long-term care is not provided by Medicare. Others are surprised that the Department of Human Services (DHS) has a program to pay for the care of an indigent older person in a skilled nursing home, but not for what is known as assisted living care in a personal care home.

Although Medicaid will pay for skilled nursing care after your parents run out of money, payment for care will be withheld if funds have been depleted inappropriately. DHS will require financial records for each of the sixty months which precede the date that your parents have run out of money. The onerous paperwork is justified by the expense of the care, which can be $100,000 per year.

The regulations withhold payment for care during a penalty period that is determined by totaling all uncompensated transfers of cash or property, which exceed a total of $500 in any single month, during all sixty months which precede the application. For example, if a parent who has run out of money either gave $100,000 to family members, or otherwise cannot account for how that money or property disappeared; a penalty of approximately one year would be imposed. Either someone else in the family would be required to pay for the parent's care, or the family would need to remove the parent from the nursing home. If the improper fund transfer is not discovered until after the parent runs out of funds and makes an application to DHS, the family's financial responsibility for unpaid nursing home bills can grow substantially while the application is being processed.

This information is intended to shock and alarm you into action before all of your parent's assets have been depleted. Several options are available to straighten out the eligibility problems caused by the sharing of family assets between frail parents and caregiving children. Nearly every wrongful transfer can be fixed, including the outright gifting of assets. As a general rule, a strategy to preserve Medicaid eligibility can be created without needing to recover assets if the amount of a parent's remaining assets is at least equal to the total of what has been wrongly depleted.

Once a resident of a nursing home has qualified for Medicaid, the family has no reason to be concerned about liability for future care. Federal law requires a nursing facility to accept the Medicaid payment from DHS as complete satisfaction, even though what DHS pays usually is less than the private pay rates. For that reason, helping a parent to preserve Medicaid eligibility is the most important thing an adult child can do to avoid being sued in the future by a nursing home for an unpaid bill.

Katherine C. Pearson, who is a law professor at The Dickinson School of Law of Pennsylvania State University, is a national authority on filial care. In one of her several published articles, she cautions that "as the large demographic cohort of baby boomers ages, thus increasing the likelihood of costly health care and long-term care, there may be heightened interest among the U.S. states in using filial support laws against adult children."

Dave Nesbit

FREQUENTLY ASKED QUESTIONS ABOUT POWER OF ATTORNEY DOCUMENTS

Often in our practice, we begin by explaining to people the various legal documents that they should have as a foundation. More often than not, most people believe that they only need a Last Will and Testament and do not understand the significance of a Power of Attorney (hereinafter "POA"). This article will answer the frequently asked questions we receive about POA documents.

What is a Power of Attorney?

A Power of Attorney is a written document used by a person referred to as the "Principal" in order to authorize another person called the "Agent" to do certain acts for the Principal named in the document.

Who should serve as the Agent? In the past, people commonly chose their oldest child, local child, or male child, but the Agent does not have to be any of these people, nor does it even have to be a family member. The Agent should be someone you know you can trust to handle your finances and legal affairs, and to follow your wishes.

What if I do not have a relative or close friend to serve as my Agent? If you do not have a relative or close friend to serve as your Agent, then there are private agencies and banks which can serve as your Agent, usually for a fee.

Can my Agent be paid for helping me? You may pay your Agent for the services that he or she is providing; however, you would not want to just give your Agent money sporadically or informally. You should create a legal contract with the Agent, sometimes referred to as a "caregiver agreement" which sets out the services that your Agent is providing and the price that you will pay your Agent. These payments should be declared as income by your Agent on his or her income tax return so that it does not appear that you are giving your Agent a gift.

How much power will my Agent have? Your Agent will have whatever power you specifically give him or her in the document. There are some powers that are presumed which are listed in the Pennsylvania Power of Attorney Law and there are other powers that must be given specifically. For example, if you want your Agent to have the power to create or change rights of survivorship, you must specifically state that power in the document.

What if my Agent does not follow my wishes? If your Agent does not follow your wishes as they are stated in the document and goes outside of the scope of the authority granted in the document, then the Agent could be held both criminally and civilly liable.

Can I change my mind about who I want to serve as my Agent? As long as you have capacity to create a Power of Attorney, you can change your Agent as many times as you want.

When does a POA become effective? It all depends on the language stated in the document. If the Power of Attorney is a springing Power of Attorney which springs into effect upon a certain event, then it will be effective when that specified event occurs. For example, if the Power of Attorney says that it becomes effective upon my incapacity, then my Agent can only act for me when I am declared to be incapacitated. However, if the Power of Attorney states that the document is effective immediately, then the document is effective immediately upon signing.

I am named as Executor of my parent's will. Is a POA Agent the same thing? No, the POA Agent acts for someone during their lifetime; whereas an Executor of a Will acts for the person after he or she has passed away. The authority granted to a POA Agent ceases to exist when the Principal passes away.

Where do I get a POA? Can I just go to the bank? No, you cannot get a Power of Attorney from the bank. A Power of Attorney is a legal document and should be obtained from an Attorney who prepares such documents.

Can I name all of my children to act as my Agent at once? You can name more than one Agent to act at a time. Generally, I would not recommend that you name more than one Agent at a time because if they do not agree, their dispute will end up in Court. Even if they do agree, however, the signing of checks and documents by all agents can be overly complicated and burdensome to the Agents acting at once.

As you can see, many questions arise with regard to legal documents and especially Power of Attorney documents. It is important for everyone to realize that they not only need a Power of Attorney, but also that the appropriate language be detailed in the Power of Attorney in order to meet goals and expectations.

Jessica Greene

CHANGES TO THE PA POWER OF ATTORNEY LAW IN 2015

If you have previously drafted a financial power of attorney in Pennsylvania, there are some changes in the law which took effect January 1, 2015. These changes may have consequences pertaining to documents drawn up prior to this date. Following are some of these changes. It is always a good idea to contact an attorney to make sure that your documents are up to date.

Section 1 of HB 1429 revised the following general provisions for powers of attorney (POAs) executed on or after January 1, 2015. The execution requirements detailed in Section 5601(b) have been modified: Section 5601(b)(1) allows a POA to be signed by another individual on behalf of and at the direction of the principal only if the principal is unable to sign and specifically directs another individual to sign the POA. Section 5601(b)(3)(i) provides that the signature or mark of the principal must be acknowledged before a notary public or other individual authorized to take acknowledgments. Section 5601(b)(3)(ii) requires all POAs to be witnessed by two individuals, neither of whom is the agent, an individual who signed the POA on behalf of and at the direction of the principal, or the notary or other person authorized to take acknowledgments before whom the POA is acknowledged. In addition, the notice that all POAs are required to have at the beginning of the POA has a warning added to alert principals about the powers the principal is giving the agent with regard to giving away the principal's property and seeking the advice of an attorney. The acknowledgment form executed by the agent has also been amended to state that the agent shall act in accordance with the principal's reasonable expectations to the extent actually known by the agent and, otherwise, in the principal's best interest, act in good faith and act only within the scope of authority granted to the agent by the principal in the POA. These above changes do not apply to a POA which exclusively provides for health care decision making or mental health care decision making.

Section 5601.3(c) addresses how an agent will not be held liable for certain acts; for example if an agent acts in good faith, the agent shall not be liable to a beneficiary of the principal's estate plan for failure to preserve the plan. In addition, an agent who acts with care, competence, and diligence for the best interest of the principal shall not be liable solely because the agent also benefits from the act or has an individual or conflicting interest in relation to the property of affairs of the principal. Section 5601.3(d) does not require an agent to disclose receipts, disbursements, or transactions conducted on behalf of the principal except in certain situations.

There are many more important changes to be addressed. So what do these changes that control financial and property transactions mean for you? Do you need to update your documents? Some of the changes may have significant consequences for your goals when it comes to preserving your assets. In addition, the changes protect third parties, such as banks, from liability.

Because the changes were not effective until January 1, 2015, they may not require you to update your documents. For example, the new requirement that a POA must be signed in front of a notary and two witnesses, each of whom is 18 years old or older, is not retroactive. Thus, if your POA document was created before January 1, 2015 and was not notarized, it is still valid; however, you may have difficulty filing that POA at the Recorder of Deeds or Orphans' Court because they require such a document to be notarized. More changes which are not retroactive include the changes to the Notice, which is the first page of a POA, and the changes to the acknowledgment executed by agent page, which is a page that your Agent (the person you designated to act on your behalf under the document) must sign. The language on both of these pages has been changed, but if your POA uses the old language, you are not required to update your document. However, third parties (like banks) may begin to assume that your POA is invalid because it does not have the new language, which will create headaches for you down the road.

Now, you may be wondering if a bank or other third party has the ability to deny your Agent the right to act on your behalf under the POA. Under the new law, a bank or other third party is not required to accept the POA if certain circumstances are present (e.g. the POA does not meet execution requirements discussed above or the Agent does not have the authority to act because of the absence of an acknowledgment executed by the Agent). In the event that the bank does accept the POA, the bank now has certain protections. If the bank does not know that the POA is void, invalid, or terminated, it may rely on the POA without incurring liability. Additionally, upon request, the bank is entitled to obtain an Agent's certification of any factual matter concerning the principal (the person who created the POA), Agent, or POA; an affidavit relating to proof that the Agent acting in good faith relied on the POA and believed that his/her powers were still in effect; an English translation of the POA if it contains another language; and an opinion of counsel relating to whether the Agent is acting within his/her authority granted by the POA. After fulfilling all of the bank's requests for information, the bank may still refuse to accept your POA if it believes in good faith that the power is not valid or that the Agent does not have the authority to perform the requested act.

There are additional changes concerning gifting and your Agent's duties that are required by the law unless your POA specifies otherwise. For example, your Agent is required to keep a record of all receipts, disbursements, and transactions made on behalf of the principal, which may put a heavy burden on your Agent, who might be your spouse. In relation to gifting, the new law modifies the power to make limited gifts and general gifting powers in a way that may be inconsistent with your asset preservation goals.

Jessica Greene

THE IMPORTANCE OF AN ADVANCE CARE DIRECTIVE

How would you want to spend the final hours or days of your life if you become permanently unconscious and are no longer able to communicate? You have the right to choose and express your preferences in advance. Inaction has consequences.

Terry Schiavo did not document her wishes for the end of her life. During the fifteen years following the doctors' determination that she was in a permanent vegetative state, her husband and parents disagreed with one another in the courts, legislators debated her best interests, and her story became very public. She died a week after a feeding tube was removed in 2005.

People differ in their approaches and acceptances of the inevitability of death. Ted Williams, a 19-time all-star for the Boston Red Sox, might be the most famous of those who will not accept the finality of physical death. He has not only had his plaque in the Cooperstown Hall of Fame since 1966, but his remains have been frozen in liquid nitrogen since 2003, reflecting his final wishes that future technology will restore him to full health.

On the other extreme, Dr. Jack Kevorkian spent eight years in a Michigan prison because of his involvement as a physician who assisted in the deaths of more than 130 of his patients before his own death in 2011. The laws of Oregon, Washington, Vermont and Montana have moved towards some of what Dr. Kevorkian advocated and practiced, as have the laws of some European countries.

Like Michigan and most states, Pennsylvania considers medically assisted suicide to be a criminal act. However, patients have the right to decide whether to accept, reject, or discontinue medical treatment. That is the purpose of what is broadly referred to as a living will, which Pennsylvania law refers to as an Advance Care Directive. As long as a patient can communicate his/her wishes directly to those providing medical treatment, the patient's wishes are controlling and override the Advance Care Directive and agent.

An Advance Care Directive prepares for the possibility that, as with Terry Schiavo, a future state of permanent unconsciousness could cause an individual to be personally unable to communicate with a physician about the care or treatment that he/she would like to receive or not receive. Unfortunately, according to a report published by the American Psychological Association, only 25 percent of adult Americans have prepared a living will. Benjamin Franklin said, "In this world, nothing can be said to be certain except death and taxes." Both are distasteful. The fact that Advance Care Directives are optional and sending the IRS a 1040 return is not might explain why most people procrastinate this preparation, which could have prevented the Terry Schiavo crisis from occurring.

If an adult does not have an Advance Care Directive, there is no time like the present to get started. An Advance Care Directive must follow a specific legal format to be effective, and a template is available on the Department of Health website. Two witnesses are needed who are not designated as agents. Facilitation of the process by an experienced third party is useful to clarify the principal's intentions and agent's options. Keystone Elder Law P.C. considers this document to be essential and will not prepare a will without it being in place also.

Just having an Advance Care Directive among other legal

149

papers is not a complete solution. Family members and treating physicians must be able to access it. The agent must be willing and able to execute the principal's choices during emotionally difficult times. Ideally, a discussion between the principal and the health care agent about end of life issues should be initiated by the principal. If you have prepared an Advance Care Directive for yourself and have not discussed your wishes with your agent, do so now while you still can. If you have been named as agent and the person who has chosen you suggests a discussion of end-of-life preferences, do not dismiss it as being premature or morbid.

If your parent has not prepared an Advance Care Directive or if you have been named as the agent of such a Directive but have not had a helpful discussion, you might need to initiate the discussion. Choose a time when you are alone together and ask permission to talk about his/her end stage wishes. If "now is not a good time," reply that you would appreciate an opportunity "soon" to clarify his/her wishes so that you will be able to advocate as he/she would want.

To encourage the principal to express thoughts and feelings, the agent should use open-ended questions that cannot be answered strictly by yes or no. Be a good listener and take notes as needed. Don't accept "you know what I mean" as a clear answer. Suggest revision of an existing Advance Care Directive if it doesn't accurately reflect the principal's discussed wishes.

The Department of Health's model Advance Care Directive offers the principal a choice of either requiring the agent to follow the instructions of the Directive or to consider the instructions to be only guidance, in which case the principal empowers the agent to override any specific instructions of the Directive.

The principal may at any time revoke or alter an existing Advance Care Directive. It is important not to allow this to happen unintentionally during the admission process of a healthcare facility. Those who have planned ahead to create a Directive but don't have it with them in an emergency room should answer the question, "Do you have an Advance Care Directive?" by saying, "Not with me, but I can get it." If you say "no" and sign a new one, the carefully prepared previous Directive will be revoked because of your panic. Services exist to help agents and principals access Advance Care Directives in times of emergency.

Dave Nesbit

MAKING MEDICAL DECISIONS AT THE END STAGE OF LIFE

The previous article discussed Advance Care Directives for end stage medical treatment. The Directive prepares for the possibility that a person's future state of permanent unconsciousness could cause the individual to be unable to personally communicate to the treating physician about the care or treatment he or she would like to receive or not receive. It is an important legal document which provides guidance, but not absolute direction, to the treating physicians.

For an Advance Care Directive to be used by an agent to act on behalf of the principal's wishes, a physician must have determined that a state of permanent unconsciousness exists, and must have access to both the document and agent. Because an Advance Care Directive does not contain clear direction to medical staff, in most instances, more specific medical direction is needed from the principal.

The Physician's Orders for Life Sustaining Treatment (POLST) is a document which translates the intentions and wishes of the Advance Care Directive into medical orders which can be implemented. A POLST may be completed by a licensed physician, physician's assistant or certified registered nurse practitioner.

Unlike an Advance Care Directive, which can vary in format or style if it generally conforms to statutory requirements, a POLST is a specific, fill-in-the-blank, two-sided, one page form which must be on printed on pink cardstock, and must have original signatures. The idea is that the POLST will be very noticeable in a patient's medical file, and travel with the patient.

A POLST form is a tool, but use of it is not required. Some physicians and facilities use POLST more than others. General guidance suggests that use of a POLST may be appropriate if a physician reasonably believes that a patient could die from chronic illness or frailty within one year. Discussion of treatment options, including those reflected in an Advance Care Directive, is required with the patient or the agent named by the Directive, and a signature to evidence that discussion is required to be entered on the POLST.

POLST is the primary form, but not the only one, to give medical directions for end of life treatment In Pennsylvania. An out-of-hospital do-not-resuscitate (DNR) order instructs an Emergency Medical Technician (EMT) not to perform cardiopulmonary resuscitation (CPR) on an individual who is carrying such a paper order or is wearing a prescribed DNR necklace or bracelet. This DNR process pre-existed the POLST form, and if such a DNR does not exist, the POLST form must be supported by an immediate order to stop an EMT from performing CPR. Without a DNR or an order from a doctor, once an ambulance has been called, the EMT has a duty to use CPR and other means to stabilize life and get the patient to the emergency room.

Without such an out-of-hospital DNR form, bracelet or necklace, the fact that a DNR order existed when someone was in the hospital does not mean that it can be considered to be a continuing order after a patient is discharged. Certainly, the Advance Care Directive itself is never a DNR, which is a common misunderstanding among those who say, "I went to my lawyer and got a DNR." This can be confusing and upsetting to family members who have been instructed by their frail loved one to "avoid heroics and let me go when the time comes."

It is difficult for a physician to issue a POLST to withhold treatment if the Advanced Care Directive is not clear, or if multiple family members are empowered as agents and the family is not united. Even an incompetent principal may at any time countermand a decision made by the principal's agent to withhold or withdraw life sustaining treatment, for example a terminal principal has severe dementia but occasionally makes a semi-coherent statement about wanting to live.

"One of the most difficult issues I face as a physician is when a patient is facing an end stage condition, and the family has not prepared in advance and feels conflicted among one another," says Dr. George P. Branscum Jr., MD, who is the medical director of several local retirement communities. "I consider discussion of end of life decisions with patients and all family members to be a good way to avoid conflicts when a patient's condition reaches a critical stage."

If the family cannot effectively serve as a patient's advocate, physicians such as Dr. Branscum on occasion can seek input from a healthcare facility's ethics committee. Such a committee includes the physician, nursing staff, a pastor or chaplain, the principal's health care agent and a lawyer. An ethics committee can meet on short notice to resolve ambiguity, but a decision to withhold treatment ultimately requires an agent's consent, if not proactive advocacy.

Life or death decisions are not easy, but advance discussion and planning is useful, if not required, to avoid emotional turmoil and family dissension. You, as a principal, should begin now by getting help from an experienced lawyer to counsel you and your agent in the preparation of an Advance Care Directive. The Directive and your family's understanding of it will facilitate your wishes to leave this world as peacefully as possible after it has been determined that you are permanently unconscious and the quality of your life has ended irreversibly.

Dave Nesbit

ADVANCE DIRECTIVES FOR MENTAL HEALTH

We have addressed the importance of obtaining power of attorney documents so that individuals may appoint trusted agents to handle their legal/financial affairs and make health care decisions should the individuals become unable to manage these details independently. Communication and decision-making about health care issues can become more complicated when mental health situations are present. Although a Durable Healthcare Power of Attorney document is generally sufficient for an agent to oversee an individual's health care in all situations, when mental health situations are present, an extra level of protection can be obtained by also having advance directives which are specific to mental health.

Mental Health Advance Directives are not available in all states. In Pennsylvania, a law approving the use of this document became effective in January of 2005. This document contains two parts: a declaration and a power of attorney. A declaration contains specific instructions for health care providers about choices for treatment involving medications, procedures, participation in experimental studies or drug trials, and the use of electroconvulsive therapy; as well as the names of preferred providers/health care facilities. The Mental Health Power of Attorney allows an individual to designate a primary agent and alternate agents to make decisions on his/her behalf and specifies whether the agent has full power over all decisions or if limitations are present. Each part can be utilized independently, or a combination of both can be drafted.

155

Certain factors must be taken into consideration when formulating a Mental Health Advance Directive. An individual must be at least 18 years of age to draft the document and must not have been declared incapacitated by a court, had a guardian appointed, or be under an involuntary commitment. There is no one specific form that must be used, but it must be signed, witnessed by two people age 18 or older, and dated. The document will remain in effect for *two* years from the date that it is signed unless it is revoked or a new document is drafted. If the individual does not have the capacity to make treatment decisions at the time the document is scheduled to end, it will remain effective until capacity is regained. Incapacity is determined through exams by a psychiatrist and one of the following: another psychiatrist, psychologist, family or attending physician, or a mental health treatment professional.

An individual can specify within the Mental Health Advance Directive when it should become effective (such as when involuntary commitment occurs or incapacity is determined). A health care provider is obligated to follow the instructions in a Mental Health Advance Directive unless the instructions are against accepted clinical/medical practice, the treatment is not physically available, or the policies of the provider (such as what is covered by insurance) do not allow compliance with the instructions. If the health care provider is unable to comply with the instructions in a declaration or the decision of mental health care agent, the provider must inform the individual or the individual's agent/guardian, and reasonable efforts must be made to transfer the individual to another facility which will comply with the instructions and/or agent's decisions.

The document can be revoked or changed by an individual with capacity at any time, orally or in writing. If changes are made, it is best to draft a new written document to avoid potential misunderstandings. In order to make sure that a Mental Health Advance Directive cannot be challenged, an individual may request a letter from his/her treating physician that capacity was present at the time the document was drafted. The letter and Advance Directive should be kept together. Another tip to help prevent a challenge is to include statements which explain the reasoning behind the preferences stated in the Advance Directive.

As part of a declaration, an individual may nominate another person to serve as a guardian should that situation arise. Guardians are appointed by the court system, but the court will consider the most recent nominee unless there is cause for disqualification.

The completion of a Mental Health Power of Attorney in addition to a declaration is helpful since not every decision about treatment can be anticipated and pre-planned. When choosing an agent, be sure to choose a person who can be trusted to follow your wishes as closely as possible. Keep in mind that the following people cannot legally serve as your agent: your mental health care provider, an employee of the provider, or an individual associated with a residential facility in which you are residing (unless the individual is related to you by marriage, blood, or adoption).

Legal advice specific to an individual's situation is recommended for those who wish to consider formulating a Mental Health Advance Directive.

Jessica Greene, Karen Kaslow

PRESERVING THE FAMILY HOME

What happens to the family home when an elderly loved one needs long-term care in a facility? This issue has obvious financial implications, but it may involve strong emotional attachments as well. In our rural communities, it may not be just about a house; instead, it may involve livelihoods—for example, adult children who are working on the family farm. A variety of questions may arise when long-term care is needed. Does a house/property need to be sold to pay for care? Can a family home be preserved for a child or children without payment? Can an older person own a home while living in a nursing home? Let's consider some of these situations.

We have frequently had clients who, desiring to preserve their family homes for future generations, took the step of adding their children's names to the house deeds. The assumption is made that when the parents have both passed away, the child(ren) will automatically receive ownership of the home. While this is true, a complication may arise if one of the parents requires care in a nursing home and Medical Assistance (MA) is going to be the method of payment for this care. By adding names to the deed, the older person has in fact "given away" a portion of the house in the eyes of the Department of Human Services (DHS), the agency that oversees the MA program. If the intention is to give the house to a child or children, it would be cleaner and more advisable to take the parent's name off the deed entirely, but only if the parent is young and healthy enough that it is virtually certain that nursing care will not be needed for at least five years. Still, our lawyers would almost never advise making this type of change.

The establishment of a trust is a safer way through which a parent may set aside property for a child or children. When a home is placed into a trust, the trust becomes the owner of the property. The placement of an asset (such as a house) into a trust is still considered a "gift" by the DHS, so this method will need to be used at least five years prior to the expectation of a potential need for nursing care. When establishing a trust, it must be irrevocable in order for the assets in the trust to be protected from the cost of long-term care. The designated trustee is responsible for managing the assets in the trust until the grantor of the trust dies and the assets are distributed to the beneficiaries. The parent may remain as a lifetime tenant of the home.

A couple of specific situations do exist in which an older person may "give" the home to another individual without repercussions when MA is needed to pay for care in a nursing home. Current regulations allow home ownership to be transferred to a minor, blind, or disabled child without any strings attached. A home may also be transferred to a family caregiver under specific circumstances. In this second situation, the older person who owns the home must have required the aid of a caregiving child or sibling in order to remain in the home for a period of time prior to moving to a nursing home. Under the Pennsylvania Caregiver Exception regulations, if such a close family caregiver has resided with the frail homeowner for at least two years, does not own another primary residence, and has provided a level of care which otherwise would have required institutional care for the older person, then the caregiver is eligible to receive the house free and clear. The extent of documentation needed to verify this care may vary depending on the circumstances. There are no penalties if the caregiver has received help in caregiving from other family members or outside care providers during the caregiving period.

When a couple owns a home together and one is admitted to a nursing home, the spouse of the nursing home resident should not have to sell the house to pay for care. If the ultimate goal is to preserve the home, we generally do not recommend that a nursing home resident remain as a joint owner of the home in this situation. Instead, for various reasons, we often deed the home into the name of the well spouse.

One of the complications which can arise if the home is jointly owned occurs if the spouse who remains in the home dies first. In this situation, when the resident of the nursing home eventually passes away, the home will become a probate asset. At that time, DHS will place a lien against the home in order to recoup the funds which were paid for care, which often may exceed the entire value of the home. This claim process is called estate recovery. A similar situation exists for a single individual who retains sole ownership of a home, moves to a nursing home, and is eligible to receive MA benefits.

Additional strategies to preserve the family home will be covered in the next article. Use of these strategies can be combined with other tools which are available to help families put together a plan to manage assets and cover the cost of long term care. Individual goals and circumstances will influence the types of strategies which are utilized. Due to the extent and variety of regulations which govern these strategies, the advice and/or assistance of an elder law attorney is recommended in order for a family to receive the maximum benefit of a plan and avoid potential costly mistakes.

Dave Nesbit, Karen Kaslow

LIFE ESTATE DEEDS CAN PROTECT ASSETS

As we have explained, using an irrevocable trust can be the best way to preserve the family homestead for future generations. The maker of the trust typically arranges to continue to live in the property and pay the expenses for as long as he/she desires. If it occurs at least five years before an application to the Department of Human Services (DHS) for Medical Assistance (MA or Medicaid) to pay for nursing home care, a transfer of home ownership to a trust will not have a negative effect on MA eligibility.

Equally important, the trust offers protection for the intended heirs, who are usually but not necessarily the children. For example, a home that is owned in a trust can be protected from divorce, bankruptcy, and creditor actions involving any of the heirs. This can limit the spillover effect of a negative event in the life of one heir creating a liability or loss for the other heirs.

An alternative to a trust is to consider the use of a life estate. Creating a life estate involves using a special form of a deed instead of a trust. The concept is simple but only on the surface. Essentially, the grantor of a life estate conveys a property to another party, reserving the right to live in the property until the death of the grantor.

Historically, a life estate has occasionally been used in conventional real estate transactions between unrelated parties. An example is when an investor buys a tract of land that the owner is not using but is attached to the house where the owner

161

intends to reside for the rest of his/her life. Such a transaction allows the aging owner to receive a windfall of cash for excess property, while remaining in the home as a "life tenant". The excess property conveys automatically upon the death of the homeowner to the investor, who is called the "remainderman."

The life estate technique can work to preserve family property in a similar manner; however, it lacks the features of protection from creditors provided by ownership in a trust. Future possible complications need to be considered if multiple children are named as remainder owners in a deed. The remainder owners will eventually take title either as "joint tenants with right of survivorship" or as "tenants in common."

If the remainder owners are joint tenants with right of survivorship, selling the property interest requires the consent of all owners. The value of the property is usually safe from a non-owner's demands during a divorce or lawsuit. Upon the death of a joint owner, the property interest goes to the other joint owners and cannot be carved out for other preferred heirs.

If the remainder interest is titled as tenants in common, then such interest can be accessed by a lien during a divorce or lawsuit. It may be freely sold to a third party or left to an heir as part of an estate. This often leads to surprising complications for the other remainder owners.

Whether the life estate is conveyed by gift or by sale is important. If the parent gives away the remainder interest within five years of applying to DHS for Medical Assistance to pay for nursing home care, a penalty period may be enforced during which the recipient of the gift may need to find a way to privately pay for the cost of nursing care for the parent. Whether by a sale or gift, the fair values of a life tenant interest and the remainder interest are percentages of the fair market value at the time the deed is created, which, when added together, will equal 100 percent. Ownership percentages in Pennsylvania are determined by the Department of Revenue, which bases its assessment on information from the federal Internal Revenue Service.

When a life estate is created, complications can occur if either the life tenant or the remainderman needs to use the home as collateral for a loan, changes his/her mind and no longer wants to live on or own the property in the future, or lacks the ability to maintain the property. Some of these snags have relatively easy legal solutions if all parties are agreeable to accommodate each other's needs. Other snags become Gordian knots, which is why a life estate is not a common solution that works for every family.

Perhaps you have heard of parents buying a life estate in a child's property and wondered how that can be a good idea. Simply put, giving a child a large sum of cash for the right to live in their home for the rest of his/her life can be a way around the five-year-lookback for Medicaid. However, for this to work for asset protection, the parent must actually live in the child's home, making it a primary residence, for at least twelve months after giving the child money but before going to a nursing home.

How much money may be given to the child in relation to a life estate transaction depends on the age of the parent. For example, an 83-year-old may pay one third of the home's value, which is a bit less than an 82-year-old may pay and a bit more than an 84-year-old would pay. Such life expectancy estimates are published in tables not unlike tax tables. They are gender neutral and without regard to the actual health of the life tenant.

Use of a life estate technique can be coupled with a family caregiver agreement to transfer more assets to a family member if care is being provided, as is often the case. Occasionally, these types of family arrangements create jealousy or animosity among siblings, especially if the "Blacksheep" sibling seems mostly interested in making sure that the parent does not squander an inheritance to which Blacksheep feels unjustly entitled. Wise legal counseling should anticipate and prepare for this situation.

Dave Nesbit

General Things to Know About Trusts

People often come into our office wondering what a trust is, how it works, and, most importantly, if it is right for them. This article will give you a general understanding about trusts.

An easy way to think about a trust is to think of it as a book. The creator of the trust is the author of the book, and the main characters of the story are the Trustee, the Beneficiary, and the Author. Throughout the story, the Author describes how the Trustee and Beneficiary will interact, what will happen to the Author's assets during the Author's lifetime, who has access to the assets, what happens if the Author becomes incapacitated, and what happens if any of the main characters pass away.

In elder law, we deal primarily with two types of trusts: revocable and irrevocable. A revocable trust allows any asset to go in and out of the trust, and the creator of the trust has complete control. An irrevocable trust allows certain assets to go in, and only certain individuals, but not the maker of the trust, may remove those assets. The terms Grantor, Settlor, Trustor, and Trustmaker can all be used to refer to the person who creates the trust. The term Beneficiary is used to refer to the person who holds a beneficial interest in the trust assets. The term Trustee is used to refer to the person who is in charge of the trust (holds legal title to the assets in the trust) and makes sure that the terms of the trust are followed for the advantage of the beneficiary. The Successor Trustee is the Trustee who steps in should the currently acting Trustee become incapacitated or dies.

Some additional basic terms which would be helpful for you to know would be an inter vivos (lifetime) trust, which is a trust established during the lifetime of the Grantor; a testamentary trust, which is a trust created by your last will and testament; and funding, which is the process of transferring assets from the individual name of the grantor into the name of the Trustee of the trust.

Going back to our example, the book (trust) may be contained in a chest with an open lid (a revocable trust) and may be completely accessible by the Grantor/Trustmaker. In the alternative, the book (trust) may be in a chest with a closed lid and a lock to which only the Trustee holds the key (an irrevocable trust). The book that you decide to write, irrevocable or revocable, should be compatible with your goals and only executed if it is appropriate to your situation. Before writing your book with the assistance of an attorney, you need to narrow down your goals. Some common goals include but are not limited to avoiding the following: probate, federal estate tax, or Pennsylvania inheritance tax, and protecting assets from a nursing home and other creditors. When you review your goals, weigh the costs against the advantages of pursuing each of those goals.

For example, if your estate is worth $500,000 or less, then you should not create a trust to avoid probate or the federal estate tax. As of 2016, the cost of probate and all of the other fees required for filing for an estate that size in Cumberland County would be approximately $500. The cost of creating a trust would be greater than this probate fee. As of 2016, the federal estate tax exclusion is $5,450,000, so if you have an estate worth $500,000 and you did not make gifts over your lifetime that total more than the exclusion less your estate at death, you will not owe Federal Estate Tax.

Pennsylvania inheritance tax is much trickier to avoid, and, depending on your situation, this may be another reason not to draft a trust. The current inheritance tax rates are: 0 percent on transfers to: a surviving spouse, a parent from a child aged 21 or younger, or charitable organizations, exempt institutions, and government entities exempt from tax; 4.5 percent on transfers to direct descendants and lineal heirs; 12 percent on transfers to siblings; and 15 percent on transfers to everyone else. If you are leaving everything to charity or to your children, then your heirs may not pay a very high inheritance tax (depending on the size of your estate); thus, for that purpose, you may not want to bother with creating a trust.

Depending on your exact situation, a trust may be useful to protect assets from the cost of nursing home care. Before drafting a trust for this purpose, though, you should evaluate your current assets, life expectancy, and health to determine if creating an irrevocable trust would be appropriate in your case. In the next article, I will go into more detail about this type of trust and lay out the pros and cons of drafting such a trust.

Jessica Greene

HOW TO ACHIEVE YOUR GOALS USING TRUST PLANNING

This article will address some very specific goals and how they can be achieved through the use of irrevocable trusts. As mentioned in my previous article, there are many uses for trusts, and they may not be the right tool for every situation. However, if your goal is to plan for the future and the cost of long-term care, an irrevocable trust may be appropriate.

It is not as simple as saying, "I want an irrevocable trust, and that will solve all of my problems." With this type of planning, in addition to the cost of long-term care, you need to consider any tax consequences of transferring certain assets into this type of trust. The main type of asset to be concerned about would be a 401K or another tax qualified account. Tax qualified accounts are accounts which are established and regulated by the Internal Revenue Code, and all contributions to those accounts are pre-tax. Therefore, if the majority of your assets are held in a 401K or another tax-qualified account, then you should not create an irrevocable trust to protect these assets—generally, you cannot transfer one of these accounts into an irrevocable trust without having severe income tax consequences.

However, there are ways to protect this type of asset. One way to preserve this asset from the cost of long-term care applies if you are married and you are well but your spouse is receiving care in a facility which is being paid for by Medicaid. If this is the case, then you would no longer want your spouse to be the beneficiary on the account because if he/she directly received this amount of money upon your passing, it could affect his/her Medicaid eligibility. Instead, you could create an irrevocable trust with specific provisions that would use your spouse's life expectancy to determine the distributions in order to avoid severe income tax consequences. Since the funds would not go directly to your spouse, your spouse's eligibility for Medicaid would be preserved. This trust could be used to pay for things which Medicaid does not pay for on behalf of your spouse—perhaps new eye glasses, hearing aids, clothing, special kinds of beds, etc.

A specific type of irrevocable trust, a grantor trust, may be used to protect your home from the cost of long-term care, but do not forget to keep taxes in mind. For instance, if you bought your house twenty years ago for fifty thousand dollars (your cost basis) and it is now worth one hundred and fifty thousand dollars, then you would have a gain of one hundred thousand dollars when you sell your home. However, if you pass away and your estate sells your home, the basis would step up to the fair market value at the time of your passing, avoiding the capital gains tax, but Pennsylvania inheritance taxes would usually still apply. You should put your house into an irrevocable trust that reserves all of the appropriate grantor trust provisions so that you can preserve the stepped up basis in your property. An added convenience with this type of trust is that it allows you to use your social security number as the tax identification number for the trust instead of applying for a new tax identification number.

Another type of irrevocable trust, a non-grantor trust, may also be used to protect assets from the cost of long-term care. This type of trust has different provisions in that a transfer to the trust is considered a completed gift for tax purposes; thus, if you survive the transfer by one year, anything in that trust will avoid Pennsylvania inheritance taxes. However, depending on the provisions, you might lose the stepped-up basis on certain property. In the event a transfer into the trust was five years prior to your need for skilled care, this asset in the trust would be protected from the cost of your skilled care in a nursing home. In addition, assuming you meet the other requirements, this trust could make you eligible for a VA Pension benefit almost immediately.

Of course, I cannot cover every single intricacy of each type of trust available. It is important for you to know that there is not just one particular type of trust that you must use; there are options, and your trust should be tailored to your goals and needs. Creating an irrevocable trust is not something to be taken lightly; do your research and make sure you carefully read the trust agreement before you execute it, especially if it is an irrevocable trust.

Jessica Greene

Do You Need an Irrevocable Funeral Trust?

An Irrevocable Funeral Trust (IFT) is a useful tool for people who are facing the high cost of skilled nursing care. The IFT is an eligible expense during the Medicaid spend-down process. It sets aside sufficient assets so that a surviving family member does not get stuck paying for the cost of burial or funeral expenses after all of the deceased's assets have been exhausted by the expenses of long-term care.

An IFT is not necessary for everyone. Persons of higher net worth, who will never need Medicaid from the Department Human Services (DHS) to pay for care in a skilled nursing home, probably have life insurance or sufficient capital resources in reserve to pay for their funeral expenses. However, residents of Continuing Care Retirement Communities (CCRC), who have been guaranteed that the costs of their care will be paid by the CCRC even after their assets have been exhausted, should consider IFTs if their assets are nearing the point of depletion.

The entire cost of the IFT is paid in advance. DHS will allow an IFT to be created for an amount not to exceed 125 percent of the average cost of a funeral, as determined on a county-by-county basis. As a practical matter, cremation expenses could be half of the cost of an embalming and burial.

There is no medical underwriting for this type of policy. The legal expense to create the IFT is paid by the insurance company, who acts as the Trustee of the IFT. There is no expense to the insured party to create the IFT other than the one-time cost of the insurance, which is the face value of the policy, which usually grows at the annual rate of approximately one percent (1 percent). There is no need to have a specific advance quote from a funeral home before creating an IFT. The IFT therefore allows supportive caregivers, who may be overwhelmed by the day-to-day details that accompany a loved one who is receiving skilled nursing care, to complete the Medicaid spend-down quickly without needing to focus on the specifics of death and what happens afterwards. For families who are facing a nursing home crisis, the provision of this service as part of our comprehensive asset protection plan is a simple process, and a relief from the need to add an extra chore to a caregiver's task list during the "spend-down process" to qualify for Medicaid.

The IFT is portable and can be used to reimburse services provided by almost every funeral home. After the Medicaid spend-down process has been completed, we strongly encourage the family of the insured to work with their choice of a trusted funeral director in advance of the insured's death. By working with an experienced funeral director to complete the detailed planning of the final arrangements in advance of the insured's death, the wishes of both the insured and the survivors can be accommodated. Advance planning with a funeral director can eliminate unnecessarily stressful complications immediately following the death of the insured.

Upon the insured's passing and the Trustee's receipt of legal proof of the death, as well as an invoice for the expenses associated with the proper disposition of the deceased by a funeral home or other authorized agency, the Trustee will issue payment in a timely fashion. If there are any remaining funds in the IFT after all the final expenses have been paid, those funds will be paid to the estate of the deceased.

The IFT cannot be accessed by anyone until the death of the insured party. The family may not borrow from the cash value. The nursing home may not expect that the value be used for the cost of care. After death, the estate recovery process of the DHS may not make a claim against the IFT to reimburse Medicaid expenses of the deceased until all funeral related expenses have been paid.

Eligible IFT expenses include the following:

- Basic services of a funeral director and staff including cremation or embalming and other care of the deceased.

- Funeral home facilities and/or staff services including management of a viewing, visitation, and a funeral or memorial service.

- Cemetery expenses including a grave side service, burial plot, vault or crypt, marker, and grave opening/closing.

- Miscellaneous funeral expenses including: a casket or urn; transportation to transfer the deceased; honorariums for clergy and musicians; stationery; flowers; reception refreshments; obituary; clothing the deceased; death certificates; and related and customary expenses.

Dave Nesbit

PROTECT YOURSELF FROM TRUST SCAMS

In 2012, I had the pleasure of going to sunny Florida, where I attended the Special Needs Trusts Conference presented by Stetson University's Center for Excellence in Elder Law. As I attended the various courses and received updates on a number of trust laws and issues that arise in an elder law practice, I overheard one of my colleagues discussing living trust scams and how we need to protect our clients.

Some terminology already defined: a Grantor or Settlor is the person who creates the trust, and a Trustee is the person who administers the trust and usually makes decisions about the trust's assets. Generally, a living trust is an entity created during the grantor's lifetime for the benefit of the grantor or another; is administered either by the grantor or another person; and is used to distribute the grantor's property after his/her death. This type of trust may be revocable or irrevocable. If a revocable trust is created, then the trust terms can be changed, and property may be removed from the trust. If an irrevocable trust is created, then the trust terms cannot be changed, nor can property be removed from the trust. Probate is the process where a last will and testament is filed at the Register of Wills, located in the county courthouse, in order to ensure that the will is valid.

Trusts can be very useful for particular situations including but not limited to: very large estates which face estate taxes or high probate fees; families who have a child with special needs; or individuals with long-term care issues and a goal to protect assets. The revocable trust can reduce or eliminate estate taxes up to a certain point depending on the situation. However, this is not currently relevant for most people because as of 2016, the Federal estate and gift tax exclusion is presently $5,450,000.

Trust scammers approach people and tell them the following general assertions which are not necessarily true: probate is very costly and time-consuming; living trusts are appropriate for all estates; this is the only way to protect yourself in the event of incapacity; living trusts eliminate or greatly reduce taxes now; your living trust will replace your will; etc. Scammers are doing this to sell these living trusts and reap large sales commissions.

If approached, here are the legal facts you need to know. Probate can be very costly for very large estates; however, for an estate worth $200,000, the probate cost would be approximately $300 in Cumberland County. If your trust package costs $500 and your estate is worth $200,000, this would not be a very economical strategy for you if your sole purpose for creating the trust is to avoid probate costs. In addition, if it is a simple smaller estate, then it should not take very long to get the notices and inheritance tax return filed. Someone cannot broadly claim that one plan is right for everyone because that is simply not true. In order to protect your assets from incapacity and the cost of long-term care, you would need to create a complex irrevocable trust that is very different from what most of these trust package peddlers are selling. Make sure that you are getting what you need by seeking professional legal advice. As mentioned above, estate taxes may not even be an issue for most people, so you should not create a trust to avoid or lessen estate taxes when you would not be required to pay them anyway. Even with a living trust, you would still need a will for any assets that are not titled in the name of the trust at your death.

Be wary when a sales person is pressuring you to buy a living trust package and is only giving you general statements as to why you need a living trust plan. Do not sign a document that you do not understand or that does not achieve your purpose for creating the document. Make sure you ask questions that are specific to your financial circumstances, and if the sales person cannot answer those questions, be leery of purchasing such a trust from this individual. Make sure you or your attorney can review the document prior to signing it. Trusts are not documents that you personally should be creating at home or purchasing online without extensive review; consult an estate planning or elder law attorney in order to determine what trusts and other documents are appropriate for you based on your specific situation.

Dave Nesbit

ANNUITY ISSUES FOR OLDER PERSONS

Annuities are common financial investments that are frequently sold to older persons. Unfortunately, the restrictions that prevent an older person from taking funds out of an annuity are often not well-explained at the time of purchase and often are misunderstood by the buyer. This article is a warning and introductory explanation that the use of annuities can result in detrimental financial consequences for older persons who need skilled nursing care.

An individual with more than $1 million in investment assets will never qualify for governmental financial assistance for skilled nursing care. Therefore, this article is not relevant to millionaires, who should be advised by a fee-based registered financial advisor, such as a Certified Financial Planner. While anyone under age 70 who does not have a disqualifying medical condition should consider Long-Term Care Insurance as part of a financial plan for retirement, such insurance is not in itself an absolute safeguard against annuity problems.

Let's begin with a general introduction to annuities. There are two kinds of structures: deferred and immediate. A deferred annuity accumulates income on the investment of capital without paying taxes until the funds are withdrawn later, usually in retirement years. An immediate annuity is a device that provides income on a regular monthly basis in exchange for a one time initial payment of capital. Ideally, this occurs by converting a deferred annuity to an immediate annuity as retirement income, executing a strategy prepared with a Certified Financial Planner.

Deferred annuities are either fixed, which provide a guaranteed rate of interest, or variable, which perform in relation to economic conditions. The ideal purchaser is one whose income is at a career peak, whose mortgage and other debt is under control, and who is planning ahead at ten or fifteen years before retirement. Such a person's goal is to defer taxes on the investment income, if not the principal, until retirement years, when income and related tax rates will be lower than during peak earning years.

When an uninsured need for long-term care in a skilled nursing care facility occurs, the demand for monthly income can require serious adjustment of a financial plan. Within 100 days after hospitalization, Medicare will stop paying for the cost of skilled nursing care, which usually is greater than $100,000 per year at facilities in our area. This triggers an obligation to pay privately until one's resources have been exhausted within legally defined standards.

Often, there is a waiting or "elimination" period after an annuitant has entered skilled nursing before funds can be accessed from a deferred annuity without penalty. The delay in receiving financial assistance while waiting through a 90-day elimination period can result in a net cost of as much as $25,000. The problem can be even more complicated if it is the annuitant's spouse receiving the skilled nursing care.

Immediate annuities also can be problematic if they do not meet the criteria of the Deficit Reduction Act of 2005 (DRA). Important DRA requirements for annuities relevant to an older person who might need skilled nursing care during the term of an immediate annuity are that the annuity must be irrevocable, unassignable, and have level payments throughout the term; be for a definite term of a period of time that is less than the annuitant's life expectancy; and have contingent beneficiary language that is acceptable to the Department of Human Services (DHS). Such an annuity is deemed to be compliant with the DRA.

When measuring whether an individual's financial ability to pay has been exhausted, the DHS's analysis categorizes money into either "income" or "resources." It is beyond the scope of this article to explain how the DHS's definitions of these terms are neither common sense nor the same as how the terms are used in the annuity industry. But when an immediate annuity fails to meet DHS regulations, it can be counted as an available resource even though it really is not. Only an attorney who is a member of the Pennsylvania Association of Elder Law Attorneys (see *www.paela.info*) is likely to understand these distinctions.

Under current law, when Medicare stops paying, it is possible to reconfigure a middle class couple's or single person's income and resources so they can qualify to receive government financial assistance before a majority of assets have been spent on the cost of care. This type of planning is complicated and should be undertaken with an elder law attorney. Annuities can limit or delay such a reconfiguration. Since the cost of skilled nursing care exceeds $300 per day, immediate implementation of legal and financial strategies often saves tens of thousands of dollars. The ill-advised use of inflexible annuities can prevent this savings.

Unfortunately, older persons are often advised by their banks to exchange mature Certificates of Deposit (CD) for immediate annuities with higher interest rates. Other times, a salesperson at a storefront investment brokerage encourages an older person to exchange his/her life insurance for an immediate annuity with has an indefinite term. In both instances, annuities are frequently oversold as "guaranteed not to lose." For many transactions, buyers should be aware that commissions paid in relation to the sale of annuities are high.

Like fire, an annuity can be a useful and sometimes essential tool, but improper use can trigger catastrophic consequences. Older persons should be cautious about buying an annuity from a bank in exchange for a life insurance policy or from an "advisor" who is really a salesperson earning a transaction commission. I am licensed to sell annuities but will only do so as part of a response to an extended care crisis plan. We much prefer to consult with a client who is seeking the advice of a registered financial advisor, such as a Certified Financial Planner, who charges a flat fee for management of the client's entire portfolio. Strategic advance planning can minimize or avoid the financial distress that accompanies an extended care crisis.

Dave Nesbit

MEDICAID-QUALIFIED ANNUITIES SAVE NURSING HOME COSTS

As we have explained, there are generally two types of annuities. Deferred annuities allow working persons a chance to invest so that investment income earned by their savings is compounded by not being taxed immediately. Immediate annuities convert a specific amount of cash into a contract right away to receive periodic income for some time period in the future.

Annuities are often promoted as a "guaranteed interest rate with no chance of losing" type of investment. That is not necessarily true. Annuity salespeople can be tempted by sizeable front-end commissions and little or no need for follow-up service. Sometimes the pitfalls of annuities later surprise an uninformed buyer, who might have been impressed by a fancy presentation made at a free dinner.

Our general advice is that persons who are older than 65 with a net worth of less than $1,000,000 outside of real estate should hesitate to purchase annuities unless they have received independent advice from professionals who are familiar with annuities and are not earning commissions from sales. The reason is that nearly every annuity either has a significant penalty for early withdrawal or a requirement for a significant stay in a nursing home before a withdrawal can be made without a sizeable penalty. Even if the interest rate is guaranteed, the cost of accessing the investment when needed to pay for nursing care results in an investment loss. This is one example of an annuity that is harmful.

Some annuities can be double-counted as both a resource and income when a person is applying for Medical Assistance (also known as Medicaid) from the Pennsylvania Department of Human Services (DHS) to help to pay the cost of care in a nursing home, which on average is around $9,000 per month (as of 2016). The DHS has regulations which limit both resources and income for eligibility. Ideally, it is advantageous for a Medicaid applicant if neither the contract price of an immediate annuity contract nor the discounted present value of future income is considered to be a reportable resource. An annuity that will be double-counted is harmful.

For an annuity to be counted by the DHS as only cash and not double-counted as a resource as well, the annuity must be irrevocable, unassignable, and have payments in equal amounts during the term of the annuity without any death benefit. The annuity must also be actuarially sound, which means that it cannot exceed the life expectancy of the annuitant. Furthermore, the DHS must be named as the beneficiary if the annuitant were to die during the term.

Few annuities sold commercially meet these conditions, which was confirmed by a 2009 federal court opinion in Wetherbee v Richman. Wetherbee was a case won by a Pennsylvanian who successfully disputed the denial of a Medicaid claim by the Commonwealth. Although the Wetherbee case was stamped as "non-precedential," it has been cited nationwide by Medicaid-savvy lawyers to benefit a spouse who remains independent in the community by increasing this spouse's income.

The benefit of increased income is achieved by converting "excess resources," which the DHS would otherwise require to be spent for the cost of the care of the individual in the nursing home prior to receiving Medicaid, into additional income for the community spouse. For example, a couple who own a house and otherwise has joint marital assets of around $500,000 could redeploy $300,000 away from nursing care expenses. Those redeployed savings would be converted with a Medicaid-compliant annuity to increase the income of the community spouse by more than $5,000 per month for five years.

One legal issue which had remained in dispute after Wetherbee was the legal meaning of the term "actuarially sound." In 2011, the DHS refused to approve three Medicaid applications because they involved annuities with terms of less than two years. The DHS argued that an annuity term of less than two years failed to pass "a sniff test."

On September 2, 2015, the United States Court of Appeals for the Third Circuit resolved this four-year-old dispute and issued a thirty page opinion in Zahner v. Secretary of Pennsylvania Department of Human Services (DHS). The federal court disagreed with the DHS and determined that "Congress did not require any minimum term for the annuity to qualify under the safe harbor." The Zahner ruling built from the Wetherbee case and was noted as "precedential" federal law for Medicaid-complaint annuities.

The Zahner ruling enables a Medicaid-compliant annuity to be used as a safe harbor for a case of a middle-class resident of a nursing home who is single or widowed. This can enable an asset preservation strategy to cap a family's liability for that parent's nursing home expenses. Zahner also offers a solution for a responsible and proactive adult child(ren) to cure an uncompensated asset transfer that could otherwise result in liability for the adult child(ren) for the cost of a parent's nursing care under Pennsylvania's filial responsibility laws.

The next column will begin where we leave off here. If you are an adult child who has a single parent in a nursing home, the following article will explain how to use Zahner proactively. It can be a tool to help a parent who failed to buy long-term care insurance or fix a financial family catastrophe caused by a sibling who, by coercion or sympathy, received funds from a parent who obtained no security to ensure repayment.

Dave Nesbit

THE ZAHNER CASE IMPACT ON MEDICAID ANNUITIES

We previously explained how a Medicaid-compliant annuity can be used to help a family manage and minimize nursing home expenses. We also reported that a recent federal court ruling in Zahner v Secretary of Pennsylvania Department of Human Services (DHS) has not only clarified the general use of Medicaid-compliant annuities but also determined that there is no minimum required term for such an annuity. This has significant implications to help middle-class families.

One benefit of the Zahner ruling is that it enables an asset preservation strategy to cap a family's liability for a single parent's nursing home expenses. A second benefit of Zahner is that it offers a solution for the proactive adult child(ren) to cure an uncompensated asset transfer which could otherwise result in liability arising from Pennsylvania's filial responsibility laws for the adult child(ren) for the cost of their parent's nursing care. In the first case, Zahner is a proactive strategy to maximize a planned preservation of family assets. In the second case, Zahner allows an emergency rescue to prevent a financial liability for an adult child.

Adult children of Pennsylvanians who receive nursing care should be concerned with Pennsylvania's uniquely harsh filial responsibility laws, which make adult children responsible for the cost of the care of their indigent parents. This liability surfaces as a crisis when an indigent parent cannot get Medicaid from the DHS to pay for nursing home care because of the parent's spending during the sixty calendar months preceding an application for Medicaid. Let's examine how the adult child's liability occurs and how the Zahner ruling validates a strategy to cure such a liability problem.

DHS regulations penalize the parent's uncompensated transfer of assets (gifts) which total more than $500 in any one month during the sixty calendar months preceding an application for Medicaid to pay for care in a nursing home. Unless a family seeks proactive advice from an elder law attorney immediately upon a parent's admission to a nursing home, since it is not possible to apply for Medicaid to pay for nursing home care until funds are depleted, the problematic issue of the uncompensated transfer of assets may not surface until it is too late. When an applicant applies for Medicaid and the DHS determines from its systematic review of five years of bank statements and tax returns that such an unauthorized transfer or gift of assets has been made, a penalty period results of about one month for every $9,000 that the DHS determines was wrongly transferred.

Unfortunately, a nursing home will often not begin the time-consuming process of applying for Medicaid until a widow or widower has only $20,000 of assets remaining in his/her bank account. At that time, the adult child who is the nursing home's primary family contact is called upon to gather the financial records required by DHS for the Medicaid application. If during the process of gathering that information the adult child discovers that his/her parent secretly gave money to a sibling because of illness, unemployment or coercion, an eligibility problem is discovered.

The Pennsylvania Supreme Court, notably in the HCRA v Pittas case, validated filial responsibility laws to enable a nursing home to sue an adult child for collection of funds due for the care of his/her indigent parent who has been denied eligibility for Medicaid. During the four to five months of the application completion and review process, the amount due by the parent to the nursing home can grow to exceed $50,000. A nursing home can't demand payment while a Medicaid application is pending. But if immediate eligibility is denied and a penalty period is assessed, the filial liability law becomes the nursing home's means of collection.

The Pittas case enables the nursing home to sue any child. The only statutory defense is ten years of consecutive abandonment of the child by the parent when the child was a minor. The nursing home is obligated neither to demonstrate that the defendant benefitted from the wrongful transfer nor to identify the wrongdoing child and join that child in the suit. Ultimately, the nursing home may place a lien on any adult child's real estate to ensure payment of the account.

Here's how the Zahner annuity can fix that. Say the responsible child discovers a previous uncompensated transfer of around $100,000 to a sibling while the parent still has at least a nearly equal amount of cash remaining. The responsible child may use a Zahner annuity to exhaust the parent's remaining resources in order to seek an immediate eligibility determination. Even when an expected penalty period is established, which in this case would be about one year, the annuity income can be used to pay the nursing home privately during the penalty period. The use of this technique could reduce a nursing home's collection issues as well as prevent or reduce a child's liability for the cost of the parent's care.

Medicaid-compliant annuities may also be used proactively for asset preservation. A parent who has $290,000 of assets and $2,000 of monthly income could choose to gift $160,000 to a family trust, which would result in a DHS-imposed penalty period of eighteen months without Medicaid benefits. The family could simultaneously use the remaining $130,000 of assets to purchase a Medicaid-compliant annuity, be eligible to apply for Medicaid immediately, and utilize the annuity income to pay for the cost of the nursing care during the penalty period.

One life insurance company deals exclusively in "Medicaid annuities" and is represented by a Midwest originator. That tandem is respected nationally by elder law attorneys who understand and use these asset preservation provisions. Even general practice attorneys and licensed insurance agents should seek experienced guidance in this area since the stakes are high.

Dave Nesbit

WILL YOUR WILL FULFILL YOUR WISHES?

A Last Will and Testament is one of the most common documents that people think of when considering the type of legal documents they should possess. This document controls assets that are in *your name alone* and don't have a beneficiary listed (also known as probate assets) when you pass away. This document enables you to have your wishes followed even after you pass away because you can choose the person to handle your affairs ("Executor" or "Personal Representative") and to whom you want to give your property. There are some important facts that everyone should understand about probate, inheritances in Pennsylvania, and passing away without a will (intestate).

The term "probate" refers to the process by which a will is proved valid or invalid under the laws of the particular state in which you are filing the will. Once the Register of Wills declares that the will is valid, Letters of Testamentary and a short certificate will be issued by that office. These letters authorize the Executor or Personal Representative to act on behalf of the Estate. The short certificate is certified proof of the appointment of the Personal Representative, and it enables the Personal Representative to access the decedent's assets and to begin administering the estate. Because of the many laws and details involved, people often elect to have an attorney assist with probate and administration of the estate. Each county sets its own schedule of fees for the cost of probate. Generally, the probate fee is based on the size of the

187

estate. For example, in Cumberland County, for an estate valued at $100,000, the base fee for letters would be $210 plus various additional surcharges and fees that may apply.

Depending on the relationship of the survivor to the decedent, state inheritance taxes may apply. Current inheritance tax rates in PA are 0 percent for your spouse, transfers from the estate of children age 21 or less, and charities; 4.5 percent for lineal descendants, such as grandparents, parents, children (includes adopted children and step-children), and an un-remarried spouse of a child; 12 percent for siblings (not including step-siblings), and 15 percent for all other beneficiaries. The payment of inheritance taxes can be made by the residue of the estate if the decedent's will is structured in this manner rather than being paid by the individual beneficiaries.

Inheritance taxes are due upon an individual's death and are considered delinquent by the state if not paid within nine months. If inheritance taxes are paid within three months of the individual's death, then a 5 percent discount will be allowed on the actual tax paid within the three-month period. Beginning June 30, 2012, certain farm land and other agricultural property transferred to lineal descendants or siblings is exempt from inheritance taxes. For additional information about this exemption, please visit the PA Department of Revenue website.

The inheritance tax applies to any property inherited by someone, not just inheritance through someone's will. For example, if someone owns his/her house jointly with right of survivorship with a child, that house will not be controlled by his/her will because it was not in his/her name alone, but the child still has to pay inheritance tax on half of the value of the house. Every state sets its own policies regarding rates and exemptions.

If you die *without* a will, your state of residence will decide how your assets are distributed and who is responsible for representing your estate (Estate Administrator). This process is called intestate succession. Pennsylvania does not distribute assets the way you think it might. For example, all of the assets of a decedent will not pass to a surviving spouse if there are surviving children of both the decedent and the spouse. The surviving spouse will receive the first $30,000 plus one-half of the balance of the intestate estate. If there have been multiple marriages with additional children, the amount received by the current spouse will be even less than stated above.

In order to ensure that your wishes will be followed, you need to execute a Last Will and Testament. This document will allow you to not only designate your beneficiaries and Personal Representative but also name a Guardian for any minors or dependent persons. Your will can also be used to create a trust for any underage or disabled beneficiaries. A will should be updated periodically due to changes in an individual's financial and social life as well as changes in state laws. If you are considering whether or not to update your will, ask yourself if any of the following four D's have recently affected you since you last executed the will: Divorce, Death, Disease, and Decade. A will that contains the necessary language to fulfill your goals can help maintain harmonious family relationships during highly emotional times of loss as well as ensure that your wishes are followed after you are gone.

Jessica Greene

ESTATE SETTLEMENT? IT'S COMPLICATED!

We are often times asked, "What is probate?" "What happens to my property after I pass away?" "If I make a last will and testament, then everything is handled, right?" An attorney's favorite answer is, "It all depends." The answers to those questions will be addressed in this article.

If someone passes away and is the sole owner of assets for which there is no beneficiary named, then those assets are probate property. Except for some very limited circumstances, in order to access and manage probate property, certain forms must be filed with the Register of Wills at the county courthouse, including the person's last will and testament. The forms would have to be filed at the courthouse in the county in which the deceased person, also known as the "decedent," was a resident. In the event that the decedent does not have a last will and testament, then the Pennsylvania rules of intestacy would control who the person in charge of the estate would be (a.k.a. Administrator/Administratrix) and who would be the beneficiaries. The probate process always begins at the Register of Wills office whether the decedent had a will or not.

Pennsylvania does not require your last will and testament to be filed at the courthouse until you have passed away and only if you have probate property. Once the probate process is started, there are certain deadlines that must be met for notices, tax payments, and filings. For example, the inheritance tax return and federal estate tax return are due nine months from the date of death. However, a five percent discount is allowed on the inheritance tax paid as long as it is paid within three months of the date of death.

Even if you do not have any probate property when you pass away, inheritance taxes may still be owed. For instance, when you pass away, if your property consisted of real estate and a checking account that you owned jointly with right of survivorship with your child, then those items would pass to the surviving owner, the child, without probate; however, the child would still have to pay inheritance tax at 4.5 percent on half of each of those assets because he or she is inheriting the parent's ownership interest. If the child was added as joint owner less than one year prior to the person passing away, then the child would have to pay inheritance tax on the whole amount.

There are a lot of intricacies in the laws that need to be managed upon your death in administering the estate. As if probate and inheritance taxes were not enough for you to consider, if the decedent received Medicaid when he/she was age 55 or older, then you may also have to manage an estate recovery claim by the Pennsylvania Department of Human Services (DHS). Estate recovery is a program that was established under federal law that requires DHS to recover the Medical Assistance costs from the estates of individuals who have died. Repayment is required for the amount the state paid, even if the individuals paid part of the bill themselves or through insurance. If you are the Personal Representative of the estate, it is your responsibility to give notice to the Department requesting a statement of claim, which is an account of all of the Medical Assistance payments made for the decedent for certain services. If there is a chance that there may not be enough money in the estate to pay all of the debts, then you can't simply pay bills as they come in. There is a specific order of which creditors get paid first.

Some estates are simple and can be administered without the help of a legal professional; however, more often than not, there are issues lurking in the background that you do not even know about! Make sure you are protected from liability when administering an estate and get professional help to assist you.

Jessica Greene

A PRIMER ON LONG-TERM CARE INSURANCE

Who needs long-term care insurance? What does it pay for, and how much does it cost? When should I think about purchasing it? The answers to these common questions are important considerations for people who are trying to plan ahead for potential future health care costs. Some reasons to plan ahead for long-term care include: the possibility that you may live a long life; the possibility of becoming frail in later years; the potential physical, emotional, and financial consequences of caregiving responsibilities on your spouse or children; and a greater chance of being able to remain in your own home or to have the ability to choose between a variety of options for care. Long-term care insurance (LTCI) is one method which can be used to help pay for ongoing health care needs.

Long-term care insurance is not appropriate for everyone. Whether or not to purchase a policy depends on your age, general health, retirement goals, income, and assets. The average age of people who purchase long-term care policies is their late fifties, but some purchasers may be in their early seventies. Younger applicants will have less expensive premiums. LTCI policies involve medical underwriting, and that's a good reason to move forward at a younger age. Someone with a chronic health condition such as diabetes or obesity may not qualify.

Premiums for LTCI policies cost several thousand dollars per year, so if you have limited income or assets, the purchase of a LTCI policy may not be the best use of your funds. Long-term care insurance is a good investment for people who have adequate resources but don't want to spend the money to pay for health care, don't want to rely on government benefits, and wish to have outside caregivers to reduce the workload on family members.

Long-term care insurance is often thought of as a way to pay for care in a nursing home, but Medical Assistance (Medicaid) is a government benefit that will pay for this type of care. There is another government benefit, available only to wartime veterans and their spouses, which can be used to pay for other types of long-term care, such as personal care homes, home health care, and adult day care. This does not eliminate the need for LTCI, but a wartime veteran should need less LTCI than a non-veteran.

LTCI is most advantageous as a payment source for care outside of a nursing home, which may not be affordable for an extended period of time if one has to pay the full price out-of-pocket. The *types* of services that are covered and *where* they will be covered vary by policy and may vary from state to state. Choose your policy carefully if you believe you might move during your retirement years.

Pennsylvania has a "Long-Term Care Partnership" program which encourages Pennsylvanians to purchase long-term care insurance by providing asset coverage equal to the benefits paid by the policy. In order for an insurance policy to be considered in the Partnership program, the insurance company must get approval from the Pennsylvania Insurance Department. Not all insurance companies participate. A person whose Partnership policy pays for $100,000 of care would be entitled to keep $100,000 more in assets than otherwise permitted if he/she needs to apply for Medical Assistance in the future. Unfortunately, unlike some states (e.g. New York, which offers a twenty percent state income tax credit for premiums paid for LTCI), Pennsylvania offers no tax incentives to buy LTCI.

Policies may be purchased from a variety of sources. Insurance companies and independent agents may sell policies in person, by mail, or by telephone. Independent agents may be able to provide quotes from several different insurance companies based on a single pre-qualification form. Some employers, state governments, and associations may offer group LTCI plans, and the federal government also offers a program for employees, military service members, and qualified relatives. Premiums through group plans may be discounted, and plan options may be available that otherwise would not be if you were shopping for an individual policy. If purchasing insurance through a group plan, find out what happens if you leave the employer or association. Will you be allowed to keep or convert your coverage? How will your premium be affected? Insurance companies and agents should be licensed to sell LTCI in your state, and rating agencies exist which can help you analyze the financial strength of the insurance companies you are considering. Each company's history of rate increases may be another factor to consider when evaluating policies/premiums from several different companies.

Sometimes, a LTCI policy may be "combined" with a life insurance policy. The long-term care expenses are paid using an accelerated death benefit. This tool will pay a certain percent of the policy's death benefit (either per day or per month) toward the cost of qualified long-term care expenses. Additional long-term care coverage which is greater than the amount of the death benefit may be available through the purchase of a rider on the policy. Keep in mind that as an accelerated death benefit is used to pay costs while you are alive, the benefit amount your beneficiaries will receive when you die is reduced.

Every state has its own laws and regulations concerning insurance, so when shopping for long-term care insurance, you may want to check with your state's Insurance Department for additional consumer information. In

Pennsylvania, the website is *www.insurance.pa.gov*, and the telephone number is 717-783-0442.

There are many options to consider when shopping for a long-term care insurance (LTCI) policy. The type of policy, how benefits are paid, amount of coverage, determination of benefit eligibility, benefit start dates, and inflation protection are some of the considerations which factor into the overall cost and function of a policy. Let's try to simplify what these details actually mean.

Two main types of LTCI policies exist: tax qualified (sometimes just referred to as qualified) and non-tax qualified. One of the differences between these two policies is how the benefits which are paid are categorized, either as taxable income (non-qualified policy) or as *non*-taxable income (qualified policy). Another difference is that premiums for qualified policies may be included as deductible medical expenses for federal income tax purposes. In order for a policy to be qualified, it must meet the following federal standards: be guaranteed renewable (the company must offer you the opportunity to renew the policy, no matter what your health status is (your premiums may increase, but only if the company raises the premiums on all of the same policies in your state); cover services which are required by chronically ill people and provided according to a plan of care prescribed by a licensed health care professional; have only limited cash surrender values; and include certain consumer protection provisions. To qualify as chronically ill, an individual must require substantial assistance from another person to perform at least two activities of daily living for at least 90 days or require extensive supervision to maintain health and safety due to a cognitive impairment.

LTCI benefits can be paid using three different methods. Most policies use the expense-incurred method, in which the company determines that you are eligible for benefits and the claim is for eligible services. Payment is made either to the policyholder or service provider of the lesser amount of the care expense or the dollar limit of the policy. Another method is the indemnity method, in which the benefit is a set dollar amount. Once an individual is deemed eligible for benefits and the necessary service(s) is covered by the policy, the policyholder is paid the set dollar amount up to the policy limit. The actual expense of the service is not considered for this method. A third method is the disability method, in which the policyholder must only meet the eligibility requirements to receive benefits, even if no services are being utilized. When shopping for a policy, find out which type of payment method will apply for each policy under consideration. The benefit amount of an LTCI policy is usually paid by the day, week, or month. Most policies define a total dollar amount that they will pay, which is called the "maximum lifetime benefit". However, some policies will state this benefit in years instead of dollars. The cost of a policy will be affected by the amount of the maximum lifetime benefit and the length of the benefit period.

There are many choices related to the type, amount, and eligibility requirements for benefits. LTCI policies may cover more than one person or more than one type of long-term care service and are referred to as having "pooled benefits." For example, a couple may have a single policy, and either individual may utilize part of or the entire benefit, or the benefit may be used toward a combination of services for both. A pooled benefit that pays for more than one type of service gives a person greater flexibility in how benefits are spent. The desired amount of daily, weekly, or monthly coverage for care in a facility must be decided on by the purchaser of the policy and should be based on the cost of care in the area where the policyholder believes services may be received. The amount of coverage for home care may be the same as for care in a facility, or it may be calculated as a percentage of the benefit for facility care. Inflation protection is an option that is available to help protect against the rising costs of long-term care. This option is especially important for younger people who are purchasing LTCI.

Eligibility for benefits will be based on specific criteria set forth in the policy, such as the need for assistance with certain activities of daily living (ADLs). ADLs include bathing, toileting, dressing, eating, continence, and transferring. A policy may specify the amount of assistance (hands-on or stand-by) which is required, the number of ADLs which require assistance (at least 2 of the 6), and/or which particular tasks require assistance to determine eligibility to receive benefits. A test of cognitive functioning also may be used to determine benefit eligibility. The start date for payment of benefits also will vary by policy. Most policies have an "elimination period," which is a waiting period from when services actually start to when the policy will begin to pay for them. Elimination periods can range from 0-100 days and may be calculated based on calendar days from the first date of service or only dates that service is actually received. Some policies may require an elimination period for every separate episode of care, while others may have one elimination period for a lifetime.

Obviously, there are many details involved in choosing a long-term care insurance policy. It is important to take your time and make sure that you fully understand the different aspects of the policies you are considering. *One size does not fit all* when it comes to LTCI. For additional information and greater detail about the options that have been discussed in this article, a "Shopper's Guide to Long-Term Care Insurance" is available on the National Association of Insurance Commissioners' website at *www.naic.org*.

Karen Kaslow

LONG-TERM CARE INSURANCE AND ASSISTED LIVING

The is the first in a series of articles which will explore how Pennsylvania's long-term care regulations have been interpreted by both private insurance companies and state agencies in a manner that can be detrimental to consumers. Regulations can be obstacles for owners of long-term care insurance who seek to make claims to enter a licensed care facility to receive help with their activities of daily living which, in some cases, may relate to dementia. Industry estimates suggest that fewer than ten percent of Americans own long-term care insurance. This compares with ninety percent of Americans preferring to receive care at home. The fact that these articles will focus on the regulation of Pennsylvania's long-term care facilities and not the provision of home care is an irony that should not be lost on the reader.

Unfortunately, Pennsylvania's long-term care policymakers have done little to promote the sale of long-term care insurance for future home care of aging baby boomers. Instead of enabling the Insurance Department to become a stronger advocate to help senior consumers benefit now from the value of the investment they made over several decades in long-term care insurance premiums, Pennsylvania's regulations have been obstacles to payment of some claims for care in licensed facilities. In addition, regulatory effort was apparently wasted in 2010 to invent a homey-sounding category of long-term care that it is comparatively unique to Pennsylvania. The poor response from licensed care facilities and a lack of consumer interest over the last five years invites present criticism.

It would be easy to digress, as in Alice in Wonderland's rabbit hole, through a maze of long-term care issues related to the challenge of providing affordable care for aging seniors. Home care is recognized as a preferred option. However, my focus will be to establish a background to understand how Pennsylvania's regulations have created confusion and obstacles for consumers.

Just what is a long-term care facility? Is it a licensed facility that provides assisted living care for dementia? In Pennsylvania, such terms are defined by governmental regulations in a manner that differs from ordinary conversation, regulations of other states, and the intentions of contract terms of long-term care insurance policies. It is generally categorized by insurance companies and licensed by most states as either skilled nursing care or intermediate custodial care for assisted living. In Pennsylvania, intermediate custodial care is further categorized and licensed as either an Assisted Living Residence or Personal Care Home. It is in this unique distinction that the problem with long-term care insurance occurs.

Governmental regulations can have unintended consequences. Such has been the case in Pennsylvania since July 16, 2010, when a new category of licensed care facility was created by Pennsylvania law. The enabling regulation (Title 55 Chapter 2800.1.b) says, "Assisted living residences are a significant long-term care alternative to allow individuals to age in place. Residents who live in assisted living residences that meet the requirements in this chapter will receive the assistance they need to age in place." Since most people would prefer not to leave their homes, using the term "age in place" as a label to describe a long-term care facility could be an oxymoronic example of government intelligence. The Chapter 2800 regulations define an Assisted Living Residence as a facility which can "develop and maintain maximum independence, exercise decision-making and personal choice." To apply the term "independent" to a long-term care facility is at best idealistic, especially when done in anticipation of subsidizing the cost.

Companies who employ home care workers to help aging persons with activities of daily living in their own homes offer an ideal aging in place solution. However, financial limitations can cause a person to seek care from a facility as care needs increase. The cost of home care can be more than double the cost of care at a similar level provided in a facility.

Over the last half of the twentieth century, Continuing Care Retirement Communities (CCRCs) emerged as a long-term care option for the most affluent ten percent of Americans who chose to age in place. Ideally, CCRC applicants choose retirement communities that initially enable their independent lifestyles and eventually support them to "age through the system" as their needs for higher care levels occur as a natural result of the aging process. Pennsylvania has a large number of well-managed licensed facilities where quality care is provided. However, many Pennsylvanians cannot afford the cost of care in any long-term care facility. Therefore, Medicaid assistance is presently available for care in a nursing home, but not an Assisted Living Residence or Personal Care Home.

When the 2010 Assisted Living law was enacted, advocates suggested that Pennsylvania should earmark federal Medicaid funds to pay for care in Assisted Living Residences as a better option than care in nursing homes. Neither the Rendell nor Corbett administrations made such Medicaid funding a priority. Long-term care expenses are budget-busters. Compliance by established and licensed personal and assisted living care facilities with the Assisted Living Residence licensing requirements would require expensive building modifications. There was no renovation subsidy offered, no proof that renovations would result in improved care, and renovations were not requested by consumers.

Consequently, only three percent—fewer than 35 of the more than 1,250 Pennsylvania intermediate or custodial care facilities—became licensed as Assisted Living Residences. The failure (so far) of the Assisted Living Residence model in Pennsylvania can be described charitably as was Ford Motor Company's production of the Edsel: "The aim was right, but the target moved."

Dave Nesbit

CARE FACILITY DISTINCTIONS AND LONG-TERM CARE INSURANCE

The previous article was the first of a series to review how Pennsylvania's licensing regulations for long-term care facilities, revised in 2010 to create a unique category known as Assisted Living Residences, have caused unintended problems. The Assisted Living Residence category neither reflected consumer demand nor resulted in quantifiable improvements in long-term care. A potential opportunity to expand the use of Medicaid in a wider variety of long-term care facilities remains unfunded.

Less than 3 percent of Pennsylvania's licensed intermediate custodial facilities now operate under the new regulations. Pennsylvania responded to licensed care facilities' lack of interest in obtaining the new Assisted Living Residence licensure status by passing another law [62 P.S. §1057.3(i)]. This law states that "no person, organization, or program shall use the term 'assisted living' in any name or written material unless the person, organization, or program is an assisted living residence licensed in accordance with 55 PA.Code Chapter 2800."

A review of the marketing materials and websites of Personal Care Home licensees shows that enforcement of this law has been incomplete. Consumers have been confused. Intermediate and custodial care facilities remain unmotivated to upgrade their licensure statuses from a Personal Care Home to an Assisted Living Residence.

Personal Care Homes offer a level of care which exceeds that of unlicensed "independent living communities", which may not legally provide hands-on care. Independent living communities offer a viable but unlicensed senior living option, which we frequently recommend as an affordable alternative for a person whose general frailty caused by advancing age might otherwise endanger or unnecessarily isolate him/her when he/she is living at home alone. Often, independent living facilities facilitate supplemental care to be provided on-premises by a cooperating home care agency.

It is an unfortunate fact that independent living communities are often misunderstood by confused or misled caregivers who seek an "affordable senior care referral" from an internet search engine or because of a television endorsement by a once-credible journalist who promotes help in finding senior "care" options. In fairness to the independent living facilities, they do not generate misleading advertisements; however, they do pay poorly-disclosed commissions to the unlicensed "free referral services" who wrongly recommend and endorse independent living facilities as "senior care facilities."

The regulatory definition of a care facility is important for long-term care insurance. Long-term care insurance should not pay for the room and board offered by an unlicensed independent living facility. However, a long-term care policy with home care benefits could be used to pay for hands-on care even when needed by a resident of an independent living facility.

Since Act 105 of 1979 and before, Pennsylvania has regulated custodial and intermediate care facilities, nearly all of which are now licensed as Personal Care Homes. State regulations (Title 55 Chapter 2600.1.b) say "personal care homes are designed to provide safe, humane, comfortable and supportive residential settings for adults who do not require the services in or of a licensed long-term care facility, but who do require assistance or supervision with activities of daily living, instrumental activities of daily living, or both."

A close reading of the regulation invites interpretation that a Personal Care Home is not a long-term care facility, implying that a licensed Personal Care Home has little distinction from an unlicensed independent living facility. This interpretation has been wrongly used by some long-term care insurance companies, convincingly on occasion with the Pennsylvania Insurance Department, as justification to deny and/or renegotiate claims made for care and assistance with activities of daily living provided by a Personal Care Home. Since 97 percent of Pennsylvania's intermediate and custodial care facilities are licensed as Personal Care Homes, this is a significant issue.

Pennsylvania's definition of a long-term care facility is not easy to find. It presently may be non-existent outside the context of a licensed skilled nursing facility. However, prior to the Chapter 2800 regulations promoting the Assisted Living Residence category, the (then) Department of Public Welfare's Office of Long-Term Living occasionally referenced Personal Care Homes as licensed providers of long-term care services. The Department of Human Services (formerly Welfare) does not have such a reference on its present website.

The problem caused by Pennsylvania's regulations results from the difficulty of drafting language about a topic which meets the needs of multiple parties. The 2013 change of the Department of Public Welfare's name to Human Services was opposed by the Department's leadership as a waste of $8 million that could have been better spent on necessary computers. Legislative supporters prevailed in the name change as a matter of politically correct compassion.

The Department's name change highlights the difficulty of drafting regulations and confining policy to terms. The same regulations are used to enforce the long-term care standards in the same rooms of the same facilities, whether the resident is paying privately at a rate of nearly $400 per day or being fully subsidized by Medicaid. A certain amount of vagueness within governmental regulations is needed for administrative flexibility; however, vagueness invites the unintended consequences of exploitation or manipulation.

As if the confusion within various regulations administered by the Department of Human Services is not enough to decipher, the Insurance Department must also consider the contract language of long-term care insurance policies written by many different companies. While it is outside the scope of this article to explain how such contract language is reviewed and approved by the Department, it is enough to say that policy language varies and has evolved for good reasons over several decades.

Clearly, the distinction when these policies were sold decades ago was to provide three categories of care: a licensed skilled nursing home; a licensed facility that provides an intermediate or custodial level of care; or care at home, which could also include care offered in an unlicensed rooming house or independent living facility. Future articles will explain how regulatory changes in 2010 and 2011 have made long-term care insurance claims more difficult in some circumstances, especially for pre-admission determinations with licensed Personal Care Homes.

Dave Nesbit

LONG-TERM CARE INSURANCE CLAIM DENIAL AND APPEAL

This is the third in a series of articles explaining how some of our clients have experienced claim rejections from long-term care insurers for care in licensed Personal Care Homes. There are a few consistently problematic issues which may be unintended consequences of the Department of Human Services' complex regulations. State regulations do not specifically define the term "long-term care facility", although most long-term care insurance policies do.

In June 2011, we complained to the Pennsylvania Insurance Department about a specific company's intent to deny coverage for assisted living care, which it defined as help with two or more activities of daily living, unless the care was provided by a licensed Assisted Living Residence and not a licensed Personal Care Home. We suggested that new licensing regulations, which made it illegal for Personal Care Homes to continue to refer to themselves as assisted living facilities, were creating confusion with long-term care insurance claims. After our extensive follow-up, the Department eventually responded a year later in August 2012.

The response said it had investigated the thirteen carriers of long-term care insurance which collectively accounted for 80 percent of all coverage in Pennsylvania. The Department said that insurance companies' practices of paying claims was unchanged since the Title 50 Chapter 28 Assisted Living

Residence regulations were adopted. However, the Department admitted that its investigation resulted in policy endorsements filed by some companies to clarify ambiguous language resulting from regulatory changes. The Department claimed that insurers operating in Pennsylvania are aware that the Department expects them to continue to pay for claims for care for assisted living services, even when that care is provided in a licensed Personal Care Home.

Since state regulations offer no succinct definition of a long-term care facility, consider a typical insurance company's definition of a long-term care facility: 1) Licensed by the state in which it is located; 2) Provides skilled, intermediate or custodial nursing care under the supervision of a physician; 3) Has 24-hour-a-day nursing services provided or supervised by a registered nurse (RN), licensed vocational nurse (LVN), or licensed practical nurse (LPN); 4) Keeps a daily medical record of each patient; and 5) May be either a freestanding facility or a distinct part of a facility such as a ward, wing, unit, or swing-bed of a hospital or other institution.

Arguably, as a matter of licensing or standard market practice, Personal Care Homes comply with these policy requirements. However, in absence of supportive state regulations which enable strong advocacy by the Insurance Department, insurance companies have required paperwork and used "confidential" results as a reason for claim denial. Paperwork must be completed by Personal Care Home staff members, and not the claimant or his/her legal counsel. Some staff members do not realize that the daily charting of the dispensing of medication is an example of a medical record or that supervision does not require continuous presence. Resulting claims can be denied or renegotiated on terms that are not favorable to the policy holder.

The Insurance Department asked to be notified of improperly handled situations regarding benefits for covered services rendered in a Personal Care Home. Subsequent complaints to the Department generated mixed results in respect to the procedure used to respond to complaints as well as the analysis and advocacy level of the Department's investigative personnel.

In one case, a Department's investigator responded promptly in writing and got a large insurance company to reverse its position and pay the full claim of an insured party who was receiving care in a Personal Care Home. But this was only after the claimant had assumed the risk of moving into the facility before the long-care insurance company responded in writing to the claim. The insurance company did not admit to the Department that its pre-admission communications to the claimant and our office had been discouraging about its willingness to pay the claim.

Another complaint resulted in a less favorable response from the Insurance Department. Despite the Department's assurance in 2012 that insurers operating in Pennsylvania are expected to continue to pay for covered long-term care services provided in a licensed Personal Care Home, the Department's investigator concluded not only that a Personal Care Home is not an assisted living facility but also that a licensed Personal Care Home is not necessarily a licensed long-term care facility because of limiting language in Title 55 Chapter 2600.1.b. The decision of the Department's investigator, who was not a lawyer, pressured the claimant to accept an alternative plan of care arrangement. The Department's investigator did not offer to meet with or interview either the claimant or Personal Care Home. The Department offered no internal process to appeal the investigator's decision. After months of being paid less than bargained for, excessive paperwork eventually caused the claimant to be relocated to a skilled nursing facility. Although the claimant's need for dementia care was safely and adequately met by the Personal Care Home, relocation to the nursing home eliminated all claim ambiguity, and it was fully paid.

Both examples resulted from pre-admission telephone inquiries to separate insurance companies. In both cases, each claimant needed hands-on help with ADLs and supervision due to the effects of dementia. The claims were initially dismissed by the insurance company because a Personal Care Home "is not a long-term care facility contemplated by the insurance policy's benefits for assisted living or dementia care." Each company offered to consider an alternate plan of care but only after the claimant assumed the risk and otherwise financed the cost of the licensed facility. These claim denials are transparently ridiculous since, when the policies were written decades before Pennsylvania's changes to assisted living regulations, Personal Care Homes were the only licensed facilities available in Pennsylvania for assisted living care.

Dave Nesbit

WHO BENEFITS FROM NURSING HOME LITIGATION?

Law firms that are not based in south-central Pennsylvania have invited the local public to contact its firm if they feel that they have been a victim of a nursing home problem. These dramatic advertisements suggest that avoidable abuses of residents in nursing homes are commonplace. The search for victims implies that money will cure the suffering and that litigation is needed to motivate nursing homes to provide the best care.

These ads are not targeted at the alleged victims, who are not likely to observe the advertisements, but rather at the families of the victims. The advertisements encourage litigation to obtain money damages as the solution to problems in a nursing home. However, once a litigation process commences, a division between the caregiving family and the caregiving facility results, and the lawyers on both sides generally advise all parties involved in the process to become less communicative with one another.

As a local law firm, we have chosen to work exclusively on behalf of nursing home residents and their caregiving families. We have never taken on a care facility as a client due to concerns that this situation could create at least the perception of a conflict of interest with our clients. Although we are committed advocates for our clients, our client agreements say that we will not discuss litigation as an option until at least six months have passed after an incident which might provoke a family to seek retribution.

We believe that during a cooling-off period, it is possible to resolve differences and create remedies which provide actual comfort to our clients during their lifetimes. If a nursing facility does not respond to our efforts to the satisfaction of our client, adequate time remains within the statute of limitations of both tort and contract matters for us to assist in initiating litigation if our client feels it is necessary. While we stop short of claiming that our clients get preferential treatment from skilled nursing homes, we believe that our approach creates a climate of mutual trust and respect so that our staff, which includes a health care professional, can effectively focus the family's advocacy to develop a care plan which achieves the best results for the resident.

It would be wrong to deny nursing home residents the ability to pursue a claim for negligent or reckless treatment that causes suffering. However, when an older person is admitted as a long-term resident of a licensed skilled nursing facility, chronic illness and related pain and suffering often is already present on some level. So, it is worth pausing to consider a) the reasons for litigation action and b) the benefits that our client could realize as an alleged victim.

The two years or more that it can take to resolve a personal injury suit can be longer than the life expectancy of the alleged victim. An alleged victim who does not live to see resolution of litigation can neither experience a sense of justice nor benefit personally from money damages, which might be what motivates the victim's family. Can a family's appetite for litigation be justified as a sacrificial experience of an alleged victim in life's final stage to improve the delivery of services for future nursing home residents? The answer might surprise you.

In March 2011, the *New England Journal of Medicine* published a study involving the Harvard Interfaculty Program for Health Systems Improvement on the "Relationship between Quality of Care and Negligence Litigation in Nursing Homes." Data about litigation were provided by five of the largest nursing home organizations in the United States in relation to tort claims against them during the time period of 1998 through 2006. Qualitative data about the level of care provided were obtained from the Online Survey, Certification, and Reporting (OSCAR) system and the Minimum Data Set (MDS), where data are gathered routinely and systematically for all Medicare and Medicaid funded facilities.

The study primarily addressed the question as to whether the delivery of a relatively high quality of care, as evidenced by the OSCAR and MDS data, reduced the risk of a nursing facility being sued. The study considered information resulting from a total of 4,716 personal injury claims made during the 8-year sample period against 1,465 skilled nursing facilities considered by the study (an average of approximately one claim for each nursing home every 2 years). The study found that the amount of litigation was not significantly lower for the nursing homes for which the qualitative data suggested provided better care than for other homes with less favorable qualitative data. The observation that litigation did not originate more frequently in facilities whose qualitative data was less impressive was true even when the analysis was restricted to environments with relatively low claim levels (e.g. Cumberland County).

The *New England Journal of Medicine* article concluded that "the results of this study raise questions about the capacity of tort litigation to provide incentives for improving the quality and safety of nursing home care. It is far from clear that superior performance will be rewarded with substantially lower risks of being sued. Policy moves that are afoot in the long-term care sector, such as public reporting of performance indicators and provider payments that are based on performance, may have brighter prospects for making nursing homes safer."

If your family member is in a nursing facility and you choose to sue that facility, it is likely that there will be less cooperative communication between you and the facility staff about his/her care needs in the future. If it is highly probable that your family member will not live to see a verdict that might create personal emotional vindication, and since a reputable study suggests that such litigation is not likely to contribute to making nursing homes safer for others, is it right for a caregiving family to truly exhaust all options before pursuing litigation? We think so.

Dave Nesbit

OLDER ADULTS AND IDENTITY THEFT

Identity theft has become a significant crime in today's society. It can take various forms, including complete use of an another individual's personal information as one's own, use of a credit card for unauthorized purchases, or use of someone else's Medicare ID or health insurance numbers to obtain services or bill for services never provided. Thieves can obtain the personal information needed to commit these crimes by simple techniques such as looking through trash, taking mail from a mailbox, or stealing a purse or wallet; to more involved schemes such as hacking into a personal computer, using medical or business records, or operating telephone/internet/door-to-door scams.

While identity theft can affect people of all ages, older adults may be especially vulnerable due to a number of factors. In general, they are a lower risk for creditors because they carry less debt than younger adults and have paid off previous loans. In addition, they have greater wealth and higher credit limits, and are less likely to check their credit reports. Therefore, thieves who use older adults' information are more likely to have applications for fraudulent loans or credit cards approved. Scammers will prey upon older adults who are lonely and present themselves as friendly and sympathetic people who only want to "help", thereby gaining trust. Older adults' greater utilization of medical services can place personal information at risk just because it is available to a greater number of employees of health care providers.

215

Unfortunately, family situations may also create increased vulnerability for identity theft if a relative becomes desperate for cash due to a gambling or drug addiction, long-term unemployment, divorce, or some other crisis.

Identity theft among older adults may be an even larger problem than we currently suspect because the victims are sometimes reluctant to report it. They may not fully understand what has happened, or they may feel shame or embarrassment about something they did which "allowed" it to occur. If a family member has perpetrated the crime, the older adult may feel guilty about turning the person in to face consequences. Additionally, older adults who are victims of identity theft may fear that others will view them as incapable of managing their own affairs, causing them to lose financial control and independence.

The potential signs of identity theft are numerous. Bank/credit card statements may arrive late or contain errors/unauthorized transactions. You may not be approved for a loan or receive a job offer as expected. Bills for products or services never ordered may be received, as well as collection calls for debts which aren't yours. Inaccurate information on a health insurance explanation of benefits form or credit report may be present. Businesses may not accept a personal check as payment for goods or services. If you experience any of these events, it is important to investigate the situation as soon as possible.

If identity theft occurs, certain steps can be taken to mitigate the effects of the theft. There are three main credit reporting companies: Equifax (800-525-6285), Experian (888-397-3742), and TransUnion (800-680-7289). Calling any one of these companies to request that a fraud alert be placed on your account will trigger notification of the other two. The initial fraud alert will remain in effect for 90 days. In addition, copies of a personal credit report should be ordered from each one and carefully reviewed for accuracy. If errors are found, contact the company immediately. Finally, an Identity Theft Report should be created. This report is comprised of two parts, an FTC Affidavit (a written complaint created by the Federal Trade Commission when you report the incident), and a police report (filed by taking your FTC Affidavit to a local police department). To report identity theft to the FTC, call 877-438-4338 or visit its site online at *www.ftc.gov/complaint*.

One can avoid the hassle and potentially devastating effects of identity theft by taking steps to protect personal information.

- Shred documents containing personal information before throwing them away.

- Do not give out personal information online, by telephone, or in person unless you have initiated the contact.

- Check your credit reports regularly. Federal law entitles you to one free credit report every 12 months from each of the three credit reporting agencies (they don't have to be at the same time). Visit *www.annualcreditreport.com* or call 877-322-8228.

- Do not keep your passwords in a file on your computer.

- Utilize passwords that mix letters, numbers, and special characters.

- Check your credit cards bills and bank statements when they arrive.

- If you shop online, use websites which are secure. A site that uses encryption to protect your personal information has "https" at the beginning of the web address. The "s" is for secure.

- Do not carry your social security card or Medicare card with you unless you specifically need it. Instead, keep it in a secure location at home.

- Drop off mail at the post office instead of placing it in your mailbox.

- Utilize anti-virus and firewall software on your computer.

For older adults who may be vulnerable to telephone scams, the National Consumers League has a Five Step process for helping them identify potentially fraudulent calls. Visit the website *www.fraud.org* and search for "They Can't Hang Up".

Karen Kaslow

PROTECTING CLIENTS' FUNDS

How can you tell when an attorney is not telling the truth? The answer, according to the punchline of a joke, is "when his lips are moving." Because of the educational and financial investment that is required to become an attorney, lawyers can take ourselves too seriously. The ability to laugh at a lame joke made at the expense of the legal community can be good therapy for an attorney to remain humble. However, occasionally circumstances surface publicly about a lawyer's improper management of a client's funds, and this saddens and concerns the legal community.

When a lawyer mismanages trust funds of any person, especially an older person, there is nothing funny about it. Because fraudulent behavior by an attorney is rare, it is dramatically newsworthy. Attorney misconduct is dealt with severely by the Disciplinary Board of the Supreme Court of Pennsylvania, which regulates the practice of law in Pennsylvania.

How can you tell when an attorney is managing funds honestly? I offer no punch line for that. But I will touch on the legal community's self-policing policies as well as offer additional precautions that a client could consider to make sure that his/her funds, especially "trust funds," are safe-guarded.

If a lawyer is holding a small amount of money for a client(s) for a short term, such as with client retainers or a real estate settlement escrow, the lawyer is not permitted to use or earn interest on the money. Instead, the lawyer must deposit such funds into a special bank account from which the interest is automatically sent by the bank monthly to a special larger fund that is managed by the Pennsylvania Interest On Lawyers Trust Account (IOLTA) Board, which consists of nine members appointed by the Supreme Court. This fund is used for various public benefits, such as but not limited to providing civil legal assistance to poor and disadvantaged persons.

Otherwise, a lawyer who is holding funds for a specific client over a longer period of time may invest those funds and earn income solely for the benefit of the client. In this context, it is permissible for an ethical lawyer to serve as the fiduciary investment agent for a client or the trust created by the client, as many lawyers have done in the course of their practices. Professional Rules of Conduct include procedures that, when properly followed as required, provide necessary protection for funds managed by an attorney for a client.

Lawyers are human, as the punchlines of jokes remind us. Mistakes and poor decisions can occur. The Pennsylvania Disciplinary Board discourages unethical behavior by imposing harsh punishment upon offending lawyers, but clients who wish to avoid becoming victims of an attorney's improperly managed trust fund may take extra precautions.

At the risk of offending a lawyer who may have an opinion which differs from mine, it could be unwise and unnecessary for a lawyer to act as the trustee of a trust, the agent with power of attorney for a living person, or the executor of an estate. Most of our clients have family members who can assume those roles with professional advice from us and other third-party professionals who have no conflicting interests. For clients who have no available family or a lack of confidence/trust in their family members, we can arrange a relationship with a third party such as a bank or CPA to act as a trustee, power of attorney agent, or executor. Again, it is possible for an ethical attorney to believe that my opinion is unnecessarily strict and cautious.

Usually, a trust that we create can be managed by a family member as trustee, although we often recommend that such a trustee consult with a professional financial manager before making investment decisions. We routinely caution our clients and encourage them to involve multiple persons and professionals in the oversight of their funds. Although we avoid allowing ourselves as lawyers to be appointed as primary trustees for clients, we will occasionally serve as distribution trustees to review and approve the actions of the primary trustee, who acts like a general manager of the trust funds. However, we are pleased when clients agree to ask independent CPAs to serve as distribution trustees instead of asking us to fill that role.

In addition to being unwilling to invest funds on behalf of our clients, we advise our clients against investing money with any fund manager who does not show credible evidence of how the client's funds have been invested with a third-party. For example, a Certified Financial Planner could provide evidence of stocks, bonds, and other assets which have been acquired. When a financial or legal advisor is also a co-investor or co-owner of an asset, such as in a real estate partnership or private investment fund, it can be a conflict of interests. When a client has both a financial planner to manage assets and also an independent CPA to prepare tax returns, there are more safeguards than if a client's funds are entirely supervised by one individual.

Older persons usually should become more risk averse and therefore should be cautious in response to investment advisors who promise return-on-investment rates that seem uncommonly high. Because of our experience with the challenges of paying for long-term care, which is a possible future need of many clients, we generally advocate caution about purchasing an annuity if an investor is over age 65 and has a net worth of less than one million dollars. Often, the best investment results can be obtained by negotiating a percentage-based fee for investments to be managed by a qualified financial planner.

If an investment salesperson's projection for performance seems too good to be true, it probably is. And that's no joke. Prudent investors should listen to recordings of their favorite comedians if they want to laugh all the way to the bank.

Dave Nesbit

SOME DOS AND DON'TS OF AGING

As we wrap up the Legal and Financial section, here is a review of some "Dos" and "Don'ts" regarding aging. Please be aware that the tips below are general in nature. Older adults who are thinking about one or more of the actions listed below should consult an elder law attorney to determine how each action will affect their specific situations. Laws vary from state to state.

- **Don't add a relative's name to the deed of your residence.** Many older adults desire to protect the "family home" for future generations. Changing the deed of your home, other than to include or exclude your spouse, will probably create complications if you need to apply for public benefits to pay for long-term care.

Do consider the possibility of using a trust to protect your home if you are able to do this at least five years before an expected need for long-term care. You must make sure that the trust is properly drafted to be irrevocable and has the correct provisions to be effective as an asset protection device without unnecessarily conceding occupancy privileges or future tax benefits.

- **Don't add a child's name on your bank account as a joint owner.** Many families see this as a method to make it easier to help aging parents manage their finances or to reduce inheritance taxes. However, in addition to creating complications if the need to apply for public benefits for long-term care arises, if the child unexpectedly passes away before the parent, the parent will have to pay inheritance taxes on a portion of his/her own money. Divorce or other litigation related to the child would also threaten the parent's assets.

  Do see an attorney to have your durable financial power of attorney drafted so that the person who is designated as your agent can have access to your account as your agent in order to write checks and otherwise help to manage your business affairs.

- **Don't assign more than one person at a time to act as an agent in a Power of Attorney document.** When two or more people are trying to act simultaneously as agents and do not agree, unpleasant and expensive court proceedings may result. It will also be time consuming for more than one person to sign off on every action/decision.

  Do appoint one individual as your agent who demonstrates responsibility and will act according to your wishes. It is wise to appoint at least one successor agent who can step in to act if the first agent predeceases you or must resign.

- **Don't purchase an annuity if you are older than age 70 or have a chronic illness (unless you have consulted with an advisor who is not affiliated with the sales agent).** If you need funds in the future to pay for unforeseen events, you could be faced with hefty penalties or surrender charges to access your money from an annuity. In addition, for certain public benefits, an annuity could be counted as both income and an asset and make it harder to qualify. Annuities have contract terms and provisions that are difficult for most people to understand, and they require little follow-up service from the sales "advisor," who is usually paid a large up-front commission.

Do consult with an elder law attorney and use a fee-only financial planner to determine an appropriate financial investment strategy.

- **Don't wait too long if you are considering purchasing long-term care insurance.** Older purchasers pay a much higher annual premium than younger purchasers for the same policy. In addition, an individual may develop a health condition that would prevent any company from offering a policy.

  Do work with an insurance agent who is willing to show you quotes from several different companies. The policy costs and medical underwriting determinations can vary significantly among insurance companies.

- **Don't pay a family member or friend "under the table" to provide caregiving assistance.** Significant family liability occurs if nursing home care is needed and an application for government benefits to pay for that care is made within five years of improperly documented caregiving payments. The government will likely consider such payments to be "gifts" and therefore impose a penalty period during which tens of thousands of dollars of nursing care expenses could become the financial responsibility of the adult children of a nursing home resident. If you have already made this mistake, see an elder law attorney immediately before the parent runs out of assets and must apply for government assistance—sometimes a corrective remedy is possible.

Do see an attorney to draft a caregiver agreement, which is a document that specifies the details of caregiving services and the reimbursement provided. Money paid under a proper caregiver agreement, which reflects a reasonable and formal caregiver plan, will not be penalized by the government as a gift.

The attorneys at Keystone Elder Law P.C. have seen how such actions, taken with well-intentioned but incomplete advice, can backfire and create complications for families. Avoid getting caught in the snare of unnecessary family drama and financial liability. Get advice about all of the pieces of the elder care puzzle as early as possible when encountering a long-term care need for a family member. Many of our wisest clients work with a fee-only financial planner, a legal advisor, and a CPA.

Dave Nesbit, Karen Kaslow

END OF LIFE

A TABOO CONVERSATION

Imagine yourself at a graduation party, backyard barbeque, or other social event at which you are first introduced to someone. An introductory conversation often contains the question, "What do you do for a living?" How would you respond if the individual answered that they worked for a funeral home? Perhaps awkward laughter or a quick change of subject would follow. In America, one topic of conversation that is taboo in social circles as well as within most families is the end of life. Although violent deaths are an acceptable norm in today's movies and video games, we become uncomfortable and tend to shy away from thinking about or discussing death (no matter what the cause) when it pertains to ourselves or people we know. We shield our children from it, use indirect language such as "pass away," and sometimes spend hundreds of thousands of dollars on medical care trying to avoid it.

Some may be thinking that this article is leading to a discussion about rationing health care. Certainly medical care is essential to the conversation. Advances in medicine have created end-of-life situations that didn't exist 20 or 30 years ago. Historically, the dying process was much quicker, and choices for treatment when one was facing a critical or chronic illness were more limited. The growth in knowledge about disease processes and the development of technology to treat previously untreatable conditions has made the dying process more complicated, which is precisely why conversations about end-

229

of-life are important. I believe we would all agree that maintaining personal dignity and respecting autonomy are commonly held values in our culture. At the end of life, these values are difficult for loved ones and health care professionals to uphold if discussions about personal goals and health care preferences have never taken place.

I recently watched a film about end-of-life discussions called <u>Consider the Conversation: A Documentary on a Taboo Subject</u>. The individuals and professionals in the film made some thoughtful observations about why we are reluctant to discuss the subject of death and dying.

- *If we talk about death, we may jinx ourselves, and it will happen sooner.* Although this statement sounds like pure superstition, this belief may be more common than we realize.

- *Discussions about death make people feel vulnerable.* Death is surrounded by many unknowns. When and how will it happen? How will I feel? Will I know that it is coming? How will my loved ones react? We are uncomfortable considering the possibilities of suffering, being a burden to others, and having an undignified end.

- *Conversation about death is intimate.* People must consider their personal identity, including values, relationships, and goals; determine what is meaningful to them; and communicate these beliefs to others.

- *There is a presumption that more care is better.* If the final outcome is likely to be the same, would you rather spend your final months and days in a physician's office or hospital receiving tests and procedures, or with family and friends doing activities that you enjoy?

- *To discuss death means to give up hope.* To look death in the eye, accept that it is going to happen, and plan for it is not giving up but rather changing the focus of hope from prolonging life to maximizing the quality of life.

This documentary was filmed by two men from Wisconsin, one a teacher and the other a hospice worker, who witnessed a need for discussion about end-of-life issues after both lost immediate family members. One of their goals is "to change the current American attitude from one that predominantly views end-of-life as a failed medical event to one that sees it as a normal process rich in opportunity for human development." Visit *www.considertheconversation.org* for additional information. Another website which offers tools, guidance, and resources to encourage discussion about end-of-life issues is *www.theconversationproject.org*.

So how does one begin a conversation about planning for the dying process? Perhaps the easiest way is to watch, listen to, or read the news. Take a current event involving death and imagine yourself or your family in that situation. Share your thoughts with your loved ones and ask them for their opinions. Your thoughts and feelings about some situations may be crystal clear, while others may be uncertain. When uncertainty exists, discussion with others can help you define or understand how others define the phrase "quality of life". In the film, Martin Welch, a physician who developed Lou Gehrig's disease, encourages viewers to think about 100 things that they do every day. If these things were to be gradually or suddenly taken away, which ones would have to remain for you to feel that some quality of life exists? What is the physical and emotional cost of maintaining these things? Both of these questions involve very personal decisions. Another option for beginning end-of-life conversations in a non-threatening manner is a card game called My Gift of Grace (*www.mygiftofgrace.com*).

When we remove the taboo that is associated with death, we can promote self-direction and dignity to our very last breath.

Karen Kaslow

Medicare Recognizes Advance Care Planning

On a daily basis, individuals of all ages are required to make choices. As children grow into adults, the types of choices which must be made increase in variety and complexity. Both internal and external factors influence our choices. While some older adults will defer to their adult children when they feel overwhelmed by choices, most value their independence when it comes to decision-making.

A number of articles in this column have addressed choices related to health and long-term care. One of the choices we have encouraged is the drafting of advance directives. While many people are reluctant to think about this topic because of our culture's attitudes towards declining health and death, it is nevertheless important to communicate beliefs and wishes about health care choices during a time when one may not be able to comprehend or verbalize those choices.

Discussions about these types of choices may take place among family members or between individuals and their health care providers. Sometimes, health care providers may be as reluctant as their patients to discuss these sensitive issues. Part of this reluctance is probably due to a lack of education about how to have these conversations. Though it may sound crass, another factor which has played a role in a physician's ability to initiate these conversations is money.

Physicians are paid based on the care that they provide, and conversation was not considered to be care—until now.

Beginning in January of 2016, money became less of an issue. The Centers for Medicare and Medicaid Services (CMS) considered activating two codes within the Medicare Physician Fee Schedule which would allow for physician reimbursement of advance care planning discussions with patients. CMS, in one of their fact sheets on the topic, describes advance care planning as "a service that includes early conversations between patients and their practitioners, both before an illness progresses and during the course of treatment, to decide on the type of care that is right for them."

Although these two codes were added to the Medicare Physician Fee Schedule in 2015, they existed only on paper as they were inactive and had no payment amount associated with them. When CMS released their final rule on all of the proposed changes to the 2016 Medicare Physician Fee Schedule, one of those changes was the approval of advance care planning as a reimbursable benefit under Medicare Part B. This means that physicians can receive payment for time spent speaking with patients and their families about different options for care and treatment as they relate to end of life issues.

How will this change affect the delivery of care? Hopefully, individuals and families will have the opportunity to become better informed consumers of health care. Just because a test or procedure is available for a specific condition doesn't mean that it is appropriate for every individual who has that condition or that every individual would want that test or procedure. Instead of health care providers dictating an expected course of treatment, advance care planning allows individuals to have greater control over their own lives. The key is this: individuals need to be willing to think about and discuss actual or potential situations and their wishes regarding treatment in those situations. Health care has many gray areas, and while advance care planning cannot be expected to address every potential scenario, discussions allow individuals, family members, and care providers to establish some basic guidelines. These guidelines can prove invaluable later on if dementia develops or an accident/illness renders the person incapable of continuing to make decisions independently.

Although reimbursement will now be available to physicians, this doesn't necessarily mean that physicians will initiate advance care planning conversations. Individuals who want to maintain control over their own care should begin to think about the last stages of life while they are still healthy, ask questions of their health care providers if needed, and share their thoughts with loved ones. Think of advance care planning as a gift that can't be wrapped. During an otherwise sorrowful time, the peace of mind that your loved ones will have when they know and are able to follow your wishes can provide much needed comfort.

Karen Kaslow

MYTHS AND MISCONCEPTIONS ABOUT HOSPICE

In American society, death is a subject which we usually avoid discussing, even though it is an inevitable part of life. Some people are given time to prepare for death, usually due to a medical diagnosis. For these people, hospice services can provide valuable benefits for both the individual and the family during an emotionally and physically difficult time. A better understanding of what hospice is and isn't can help alleviate the sense of dread that is often felt when this word is mentioned.

Myth: Hospice means an individual is "giving up" and that death is imminent.
Hospice care is designed to provide people who have approximately six months or less to live with the services and support they need to maximize the quality of that time. The goals of care change from trying to cure the disease or lengthen the lifespan to achieving physical comfort and emotional acceptance.

Myth: Hospice is a place.
While there is one hospice in our area that is an actual building (the Carolyn Croxton Slane Residence in Harrisburg, operated by Hospice of Central PA), the word hospice actually means a philosophy of care.

Myth: Hospice is only for cancer patients.
Hospice staff also care for individuals with advanced dementia or chronic diseases such as heart, lung, kidney, and

neuromuscular conditions. More than 60 percent of hospice clients have diagnoses other than cancer.

Myth: Hospice provides 24-hour care.
Hospice workers include nursing assistants, nurses, social workers, and chaplains. Their visits to provide care can range from once or twice a week to daily, depending on the individual's needs. Visits are usually no more than a couple of hours in length.

Myth: Hospice means I'm going to be given additional drugs which will hasten my death.
Hospice workers desire to find the correct combination of medications in the lowest doses possible which will be effective in controlling an individual's symptoms without undesirable side effects.

Myth: Hospice only provides care in a private home.
Hospice will provide care wherever a client calls home, whether it be a private home, personal care home, nursing home, apartment, or even under a bridge.

Myth: Hospice care is expensive.
If clients have Medicare or Medicaid, hospice benefits are covered 100 percent. For individuals with private insurance, hospice staff can review your plan to determine coverage levels and potential out-of-pocket costs.

Myth: A doctor is the only one who can make a decision about hospice.
Individuals and families can speak with hospice staff at any time to determine if services may be appropriate for their loved one. If your physician hasn't mentioned hospice, do not be afraid to initiate the discussion, as a physician's order is required before any care can be provided.

Myth: **Hospice patients can't go to the hospital or receive specialized treatments.**

While hospice attempts to manage an individual's symptoms in the "home" setting, sometimes a short term hospitalization may improve care. Treatments which are usually viewed as curative (such as chemotherapy or blood transfusions) may be appropriate for hospice clients if they are given to provide comfort.

These are only some of the myths that the professionals who provide hospice services are trying to overcome in their efforts to better serve individuals and families near the end of life. These myths were shared by Heartland and Homeland Hospices, two of a number of companies in our area that provide this type of service. Individuals have the right to choose any hospice provider they desire. Heartland has heard from families many times that they wish they had started services sooner. Don't let one of these myths result in a delay of additional support and care for your loved one.

Karen Kaslow

A FINAL GIFT

Have you been faced with a long list of detailed decisions to make after the death of a loved one while also trying to grieve? This dilemma often confronts families when a loved one dies without having discussed preferences related to funeral planning. Families are faced with quickly choosing a funeral home, cemetery, burial or cremation, casket, flowers, music, and clothing, as well as gathering details for an obituary, notifying family and friends, and paying for these considerable expenses. It is a tremendous final gift to one's family when an individual takes the time to think about and pre-plan for some of these details. Pre-planning allows for decisions to be made without the stress of grief and with plenty of time to consider choices.

An understanding of some of the procedures that funeral homes follow may help decrease a fear of pre-planning. If death has occurred at a hospital or other health care facility, the facility will contact the funeral home after receiving approval from the family. If a death occurs at home, family members should call 9-1-1 if the death is unexpected or there is any uncertainty; the hospice nurse if hospice was providing care for the individual; or they may call the funeral home directly, and the funeral home will contact the coroner. When a funeral home receives a body, the first step is to fully wash the body, including the hair and nails. The funeral home must obtain permission from the next of kin to proceed with embalming, which is the process used to restore a natural lifelike appearance to the body and to preserve the body. An embalming is only required when a public viewing is planned or if a body will be transported across state lines. The process is fairly simple and involves circulating embalming fluid through the body while the blood is drained. This is accomplished with equipment similar to an intravenous line, and uses a pump or gravity to circulate the fluid. Jill Lazar, Preneed Counselor and Funeral Director at Hoffman-Roth Funeral Home in Carlisle, advises that embalming be completed if the funeral home will be holding the body for an extended period of time and/or to make a family viewing more comfortable, especially if children are going to attend. "An embalming (and restoration if necessary) may be what a family needs for closure. Seeing their loved one looking peaceful after a lengthy illness or unexpected death may have lasting psychological benefits for survivors long after the individual has been viewed."

One of the major decisions which must be made is traditional burial or cremation. Jill estimates that the current trend is a 50/50 split between these two choices, with most who choose cremation having their ashes buried afterward. In some states, a family is required to identify the body at the crematory; but this is not the case in PA. It is a requirement, however, that a crematory hold a body for at least 24 hours prior to cremation taking place. Some funeral homes provide crematory services onsite. With cremation, an individual can still choose to have embalming, a viewing, and a funeral service; however, burial of the ashes at the cemetery is more likely to involve only family. In opposition, after a traditional funeral, a larger number of people also visit the cemetery for the burial.

When people hear the news of the death of someone they knew, their initial response may be to question the details of the death and plans for a service. Attending a service is one way for the community to show support for a family's loss and for individuals to begin to experience closure. If there is a delay in scheduling a service, families may experience less external support because members of the general community will move on. Grieving family members may receive more telephone calls during a time when they may have less energy and inclination to speak with people if service arrangements are not included in an obituary.

When planning a funeral/memorial service, it is important to consider the needs of the survivors as well as honor the wishes of the deceased. Couples who discuss funeral planning ahead of time may find that they have different ideas about what they each want. At the time of death, the survivor is more likely to be accepting of arrangements that differ from personal ideals if discussion has been held beforehand. When an individual completes prearrangements, he/she can change those plans at any time, but family members cannot change prearrangements at the time of death. When prepayment is made, the funds may be irrevocable, and should changes be made later on for less expensive arrangements, a refund cannot be paid until the time of death.

While a sense of discomfort about death may prevent some people from considering funeral pre-planning, concerns about the cost may be a deterrent to others. Funeral planning can be expensive, but pre-planning allows individuals time to consider a budget when making decisions about desired plans and services. The costs for some services may be guaranteed at the time of pre-planning and payment, while others are estimates which may change by the time the services are actually utilized. Whether or not funeral planning is completed ahead of time, it is important for individuals to be honest and realistic with themselves and the funeral home about the size of the financial commitment that can be made for these services.

When pre-planning, check with the funeral director as to whether or not a price guarantee can be provided for certain services. Funeral homes are required by law to establish a general price list for their services, and these services are the ones which some funeral homes will guarantee, such as costs for a casket or urn, embalming, vault, cremation, a private or public service at the funeral home or in a church, and transportation of the body. Other costs which can be estimated, but are not controlled by the funeral home (and thus cannot be guaranteed) include death certificates; flowers; obituaries; church staff including clergy, musicians, and custodians; the coroner's fee; and the opening and closing of a grave.

When pre-payment for services is made, a funeral home should place the funds in an irrevocable and transferrable insurance product to protect the investment. This is important in case the funeral home should go out of business or the client move out of the area and/or desire to utilize a different funeral home in the future. Some funeral homes will accept a life insurance policy as payment for services. One option is to assign the entire policy to the funeral home. Then, at the time of death, if there are extra funds after all services are paid for, the funeral home will reimburse the family. A second option is a partial assignment of the policy, in which the insurance company pays the funeral home at the time of death, and then pays the remainder of the policy to the beneficiaries. Most funeral homes will not provide a price guarantee for pre-planned funerals when a pre-existing life insurance policy will be utilized as payment for services. Monthly payment plans may also be available if one cannot afford to pay the entire cost at once. A discussion about general wishes for services and available payment options held prior to decisions about specific products and services can help a funeral director assist a client more compassionately and effectively.

For those who are budget-conscious, there are some ways to reduce the expenses associated with funeral planning. Some of the most obvious include the type of casket or urn and the flowers which are chosen. In general, the cost of cremation is less expensive than the cost of a traditional burial.

Newspapers, which at one time didn't charge for obituaries, now charge by the line, and a $400-$500 fee for this service is not uncommon. The type of cemetery utilized can also influence costs. Large cemeteries which are owned by corporations have more regulations and thus will charge more for the cost of the grave itself as well as its opening and closing. Smaller cemeteries and church owned cemeteries tend to be more flexible and, in many cases, less expensive.

If you remain uncomfortable with the thought of planning the details of your own funeral or are unsure about discussing plans with a specific funeral home, an irrevocable funeral trust can be used to set funds aside to cover this expense. These trusts have several benefits, including protection from the cost of long-term care (your family won't have to pay for your funeral if all of your personal assets have been used to pay for care in a facility), they can be used at almost any funeral home, and they are an eligible expense for a Medical Assistance spend-down (check with an elder law attorney about certain regulations which may apply).

Karen Kaslow

COMFORT AT THE END OF LIFE

Are you reluctant to face the thought of death? Fear, anger, and inadequacy are some common feelings we experience when we must deal with our own or a loved one's mortality. An understanding of how to help comfort someone who is at the end of life can help us cope with these feelings, and it allows us to provide more effective care for those in need of our support. In its literature about the end of life, the National Institute on Aging discusses four main areas of comfort which should be addressed at that time: mental and emotional, spiritual, practical, and physical. Hospice and palliative care are two types of services that attempt to identify and meet these comfort needs for the individuals and families with whom they interact. However, you don't have to be a professional to learn how to comfort someone who is near death.

Let's start with mental/emotional comfort. Everyone will have his/her own experience with death, and there is no right or wrong way to think or feel about it. People are often afraid of talking about death and don't know what to say to someone who is dying. They try to offer platitudes, which, although meant well, usually aren't helpful. Instead, let the individual know that you are willing to listen, and allow them to guide the conversation. Some people may be willing to share their thoughts while others may not be ready. Don't be offended if the individual chooses someone else with whom to talk; sometimes, sharing thoughts and feelings with family or friends can be more difficult than sharing them with a more "neutral" party, such as a medical professional. Dying people may have specific fears or concerns, such as being alone at the time of death, or leaving others behind. Some fears and concerns (like the two aforementioned) may be common among those who are dying, while others may be highly individualized. It is important not to assume that you know what someone's fears are or impose your own fears on the individual. These situations may lead to misunderstandings and tension instead of comfort. A dying individual will be comforted when his or her own fears and concerns are validated and attempts are made to address them, no matter how trivial they may seem to others. Meeting these needs will allow the individual to relax and focus his/her energy and attention on important relationships.

Other mental/emotional needs revolve around the environment. How many visitors does the individual feel comfortable with at one time? What about lighting and noise levels? Absolute quiet might not be necessary; the noise of daily activity may be reassuring. Background music may or may not be appreciated. Thinking about your loved one's personality can help guide routines and activities. Those who are dying but still relatively active will appreciate being treated "normally", and they may have need for time alone. Respecting the individual's ability to make choices and retain autonomy for as long as possible is also an important factor in promoting well-being.

Understanding an individual's spiritual needs will also contribute to his/her level of comfort. The belief that one's life has been meaningful provides a sense of peace to many people. This can be reinforced by sharing memories, verbalizing the importance of your relationship with the dying person, discussion about personal beliefs and faith, and prayer. If loved ones are distant and unable to visit in person, these activities can be shared through letters, recordings, and even Skype. When speaking with the dying individual, asking

245

open ended questions about beliefs, meaningful experiences, and regrets can help initiate a discussion of potentially sensitive topics. Sharing tears can be cleansing for everyone. Writing down information that is shared verbally may become a source of comfort to family members and friends after the individual's death. To achieve a sense of closure, the individual may require assistance to make telephone calls or write letters to others to say thank you, offer an apology, ask for forgiveness, or say goodbye.

Providing comfort for the latter two needs often focuses on what others *say* to the individual and family. On the other hand, addressing practical tasks and physical condition focuses on what others can *do* to help meet needs. Practical tasks are those everyday responsibilities that keep a home and family running smoothly. These tasks may become a source of worry for a dying individual, especially if they are tasks that the individual was accustomed to performing. Questions may arise about who will take care of these tasks now, or when and how the tasks will be taken care of. Determining what the individual's concerns are and helping develop a plan to complete these responsibilities can be reassuring for the individual. Family members may feel overwhelmed by even simple tasks when they are dealing with feelings of grief and loss. Assistance with daily chores can be a great source of comfort for both the individual and family. It is most effective, however, to be specific when offering help. Being specific allows the family to say yes or no quickly instead of having to devote time or energy to finding a task that is "suitable" for the volunteer. Examples of practical tasks include running errands, washing or folding laundry, preparing a meal, or making telephone calls. If you are the caregiver, don't be afraid to ask others for help or to assign a specific task when someone offers assistance.

Physical condition is perhaps the most common factor that is thought of in relation to comfort, and pain is at the top of the list. Keep in mind that pain is easier to prevent than to treat, and treatment measures are more effective at the beginning stages of pain rather than once it has become more severe. A variety of medications and doses may need to be tried before the most effective one (with the fewest side effects) is discovered. Increased muscle tension may be an indication of pain for someone who is unable to verbalize it. Another sign of discomfort is related to temperature, as temperature sensitivity may increase in a dying individual, and simply adding or removing a blanket can improve comfort. Breathing patterns may also change at the end of life, and the use of oxygen or a cool mist humidifier can promote easier breathing. A fan may be needed to ensure adequate ventilation, and the individual's position will also affect the breathing pattern. Skin irritation can occur easily in an individual who cannot change position independently. Keeping the skin clean and dry, using extra cushioning, and regular mouth care are effective ways of preventing skin irritation. The expectation and management of increased fatigue will be important for those trying to live as "normally" as possible. Allowing extra time for the completion of activities, planning for rest periods in between them, and finding creative ways to perform activities while expending less energy will reduce both physical and emotional stress.

The role of nutrition and hydration at the end of life can be a controversial issue for many people in relation to physical comfort. When an individual is near the end of life, families may feel concerned about the effects of decreased appetite or an absence of food/fluid intake. As healthy people, we experience sensations of hunger and thirst as signals from our bodies that nutrients and fluids are needed to maintain energy levels and promote normal functioning of our cells, tissues, and organs. Some people automatically assume that these sensations continue to be experienced at the end of life and that the lack of food and fluids causes pain and discomfort. "Starvation" and dehydration are viewed as cruel ways to die, and questions about intravenous fluids and tube feedings can lead to mixed emotions and disagreements among individuals, families, and medical professionals.

However, at the end of life, the body does not continue to function in the same way as in a healthy individual. During the dying process, a loss of appetite is a normal occurrence as the body naturally begins to slow down. As our bodily systems (such as the digestive, circulatory, respiratory, and muscular systems) utilize fewer nutrients, sensations of hunger are lessened. The ability to swallow food may become difficult or impaired, leading to discomfort when attempting to eat and increasing the risk of aspiration (food particles getting into the lungs instead of the digestive system). Aspiration places people at risk for pneumonia. Other symptoms such as nausea, vomiting, and constipation may occur, and food intake may serve only to aggravate these symptoms. As saliva production decreases, the sensation of taste may be altered, which can reduce an individual's desire to eat. Nutrition provided via a feeding tube may not improve symptom control or even lengthen life as the body may not be capable of absorbing or using the nutrients. At the end of life, the focus of food intake should be for the enjoyment of the individual, not for the purpose of nutrition. Small portions of favorite foods as requested by the individual are the most effective method of giving comfort at this time.

Another misperception at the end of life is that the lack of sufficient fluid intake can cause discomfort. While thirst is an indicator of the body's need for fluids, at the end of life, the sensation of thirst is more often associated with a dry mouth. Frequent mouth care can help alleviate this symptom. Avoid using flavored swabs as they may be irritating to sensitive tissues in the mouth, and if the individual is on oxygen, be sure to use lip balm that isn't petroleum-based. Artificial saliva may also be used to reduce dryness in the mouth. Individuals who are conscious and not at risk of aspiration may enjoy ice chips. As the body begins to naturally dry out, watch for dryness of the eyes. Artificial tears, eye lubricant, and moist washcloths over the eyes can help promote comfort.

When oral intake is poor or not recommended, the use of intravenous fluids may be thought of as a method of preventing dehydration. In a dying individual, intravenous fluids may cause more harm than good. First is the discomfort and potential for infection related to maintaining an access to administer the fluids. The body may be unable to effectively process the fluids, leading to swelling in various areas of the body. Intravenous fluids will increase the amount of secretions an individual has, resulting in coughing spells and/or shortness of breath. Lastly, fluid that goes in will also cause the bladder to fill. Fatigue and physical pain may make toileting difficult, or the individual may be incontinent and experience discomfort with the frequent skin care needed to prevent breakdown. A catheter may take care of the incontinence issue but is also another potential source of infection in addition to a cause of discomfort during its insertion. When allowed to dry out naturally, normal chemical changes in the body and brain may produce a mild euphoria and improve an individual's comfort level. This euphoria may allow for lower doses of narcotics or other medications, thus reducing the side effect of increased sedation and allowing for more quality time with loved ones. Does dehydration still sound cruel?

When considering the physical and psychosocial issues associated with food and fluid intake, bear in mind that the body's inability to process food and fluids at the end of life is the result of advanced age, a disease process, or a traumatic injury. One or a combination of these three conditions becomes the cause of death, not the lack of food or fluids. The use of tube feedings and intravenous fluids may give an individual a little more time on this earth, but at what price? Individuals, families, and health care providers can benefit from open and honest discussions about personal preferences for care prior to the onset of the end of life. Not all situations are black or white, however, and sometimes the end of life is unpredictable. Education about the potential risks and benefits associated with the issues of food and fluid intake can help you be better prepared in case you need to make difficult decisions for yourself or a loved one. Ultimately, these discussions and education will help you provide better comfort on all four levels for your loved one at the end of life.

Karen Kaslow

SAFETY

A User-Friendly Home

Are you nearing retirement and thinking about purchasing a different home for your retirement years? Perhaps you've lived in "the family home" for a long time and are wondering if any modifications or repairs should be made to accommodate potential mobility or cognition changes as you age. Maybe you are an adult child considering the possibility of mom or dad, or maybe both, moving in. An obvious factor to consider is the presence of steps (both inside and outside the home). But there are additional less obvious details which can make a home more user-friendly for an older adult or individual with physical or cognitive challenges. Some of these details can be easily remedied by the purchase of adaptive equipment, but others involve more expensive structural changes. Following are some general safety and room-by-room details to consider.

General Safety

- Indoor and outdoor steps should have sturdy handrails.

- Steps that can be potentially slippery (hardwood or painted) may benefit from having nonskid strips applied near the edges. For those who have visual impairments, the strips should be a color that contrasts with the color of the steps.

- Light switches should be located near all entrances to each room, at each end of hallways, and at the top and bottom of stairwells.

- Lighting should be bright enough throughout the home but without glare.

- Lever handles are easier to operate than doorknobs.

- Interior doors should have locks which can be opened from either side.

- Hallways and doorways should be wide enough to accommodate a walker or wheelchair (keep in mind the angle needed to turn a wheelchair to move through each doorway).

- The water heater should be set at 120 degrees to reduce the risk of scalding. However, check the dishwasher first, as some may require a water temperature of 140 degrees for optimum cleaning.

- Solid color carpeting that has a dense pile will reduce the risk of falls. Deep pile carpeting can be more difficult to walk on, and patterned carpeting may cause optical illusions and be troublesome for those who have difficulty with depth perception.

- To lower the fall risk on hardwood floors, avoid wax, high gloss polishes, and throw rugs.

- Room entrances should not have raised door thresholds.

- Smoke alarms and carbon monoxide detectors should be present near all sleeping areas.

Kitchen

- Check that cabinets and countertops are at a comfortable height and that there is space to roll a wheelchair under a counter if needed.

- Harder to reach cabinets could have a pull-out design, and lower cabinets could have drawers instead of shelves.

- A side-by-side refrigerator/freezer will be easier to use than a top-bottom model.

- Oven controls should be located on the front of the oven, and knobs or touch pad controls should be easy to understand and manage.

- A preferred stove design has a cooking surface that works by induction, which prevents the surface from becoming hot, and can be installed like a countertop so that a wheelchair can roll under it.

- Electric or gas stoves should not be positioned under a window because the presence of curtains will increase the risk of fire.

- The sink should have a single-lever mixing faucet.

- The touch pad of a microwave should be large and easy to read, and the microwave should be in a convenient location. A microwave mounted over a stove may increase the risk of injury if both appliances are used at the same time.

Bathroom

- There should be one located on the main floor of the home as well as near the bedroom (if the home is multi-level).

- Grab bars should be present or can be installed near the toilet and tub/shower.

- Check that the toilet is a comfortable height.

- It is recommended that the tub/shower has a hand-held spray unit and a built-in seat or space to utilize a shower chair (chairs are available which extend over the side of a tub if a stall shower is not present; however, you will need a curtain instead of shower doors to minimize water escape).

- Sink and tub/shower controls should have lever handles, preferably single mixing ones.

- A pedestal sink may be needed if a wheelchair or regular chair will be used in front of it

- Countertops and a mirror should be the appropriate height or able to tilt if someone will be sitting during grooming.

- The size of the bathroom should be adequate for wheelchair maneuverability.

- Avoid throw rugs and bathmats. The floor should be carpeted (low pile) or matte-finished, textured tile instead of a smooth, potentially slippery surface.

- Towel racks and built in soap dishes should be secure and not located where they might be used as a grab bar.

Bedroom

- One should be available on the main floor of the home.

This list is by no means exhaustive, and homes meeting all or most of these considerations may be difficult to find. Home design is the key; after all, modifications are easier to make than physical alterations should one's health status change and the need for adaptations arise.

Karen Kaslow

ARE YOU "BANKING" FOR A HEALTHIER FUTURE?

Do your joints ache or your bones creak? Does your back complain when you get out of bed in the morning? I asked some local physical therapists for tips on helping older adults (and those of us who are working on becoming older) be safer and healthier. My sister, a physical therapist in Connecticut, said it this way, "The most common thing I hear from people in hospitals is 'I never thought I'd get this way.' We hope not to lose our jobs, but we keep money in the bank just in case. We hope never to be sick, but we should keep strength in the "bank" of our bodies JUST IN CASE." The following health and safety tips were shared by my sister, and therapists from Green Ridge Village in Newville, and Cumberland Crossings Retirement Community in Carlisle. We appreciate their willingness to share their expertise.

The most common theme among the tips I received was to be active. Folks who have been physically active tend to recover from injuries and illnesses more quickly than those who haven't. Physical activity doesn't have to be strenuous - any activity that keeps your body moving will be helpful, even household chores. If you are interested in starting an exercise routine, you will be more successful if you choose something you will enjoy and are able to make it a part of your daily routine. It usually takes about six months for a change to become routine, so don't give up, even though it may feel difficult in the beginning. Simple changes like choosing a parking space that is farther away or taking the stairs instead of the elevator can be an easy way to start exercising more. Planning an activity with a friend can help provide needed encouragement and motivation. Exercise programs designed for older adults, conducted by local senior centers or the YMCA, can provide opportunities to form new friendships in addition to the physical benefits of each program.

Increasing your physical activity is a great way to start down the road to better health, but remember to check with your physician before making any drastic changes. If you are already experiencing loss of strength or movement, or if you have pain, your physician can order a physical therapy consult to help determine the type of activities which would be most beneficial for you. The sooner you treat your symptoms, the greater the benefit you will receive.

Whether or not you plan to exercise, there are a couple of things that everyone can do to help their bodies. Gentle stretching before getting out of bed in the morning and before exercise will reduce discomfort and allow your muscles and joints to "wake up" before they are put to work. Have you taken a look at your feet lately? What type of shoes are you wearing? Many of today's footwear styles lack the support that is necessary for proper balance and healthier joints. Just by changing your shoes you may be able to improve your endurance and reduce those aches and pains.

Here are some other tips to help you with your new "bank account:"

- When you are ready to get up from a seated position, you will have better balance if you lean forward until you have "nose over toes" - then stand up.

- Remove area rugs from your home and reduce clutter. Both create tripping hazards.

- When walking up and down stairs, remember "the good go to heaven, the bad go to hell."

(When going up, lead with the stronger leg. When coming down, lead with the weaker one.)

- Take your time. Most falls are caused by rushing.

- Intersperse strenuous activities with lighter ones to reduce fatigue and take rest breaks when you are tired.

- Utilize good body mechanics to help reduce pain and risk of injury. For example, use your leg muscles to lift, and keep the item you are lifting close to your body.

- A diet with fewer processed foods and more fresh fruits, vegetables, and meat can improve your overall health and functioning.

- Don't be afraid to ask for help when you need it!

Although there are some things which we cannot control in life, we do have the ability to make choices which will positively affect our health. Some choices may require more effort than others, but in the long run, isn't feeling better worth it? A therapist from Cumberland Crossings shared one final tip: "Take time each day to be thankful for all the wonderful things life has to offer, and prepare to be amazed at how much more you will enjoy your life to the fullest."

Karen Kaslow

RED FLAGS FOR AN OLDER ADULT'S INDEPENDENCE

Do you have elderly loved ones who are still living independently in their own homes? Are you questioning their ability to do so safely? While some clues to changes in an older adult's level of functioning may be readily apparent, others may be more subtle. Following are some clues to look for which might indicate that your loved one may require additional help at home or would benefit from a move to a care facility.

Physical signs, such as changes in grooming habits, are often the ones that are the most obvious to families. One may notice that the individual is not combing his/her hair, is wearing wrinkled or stained clothing, or has developed body odor. Changes in strength, balance, or endurance may be evidenced by difficulty getting out of a chair, holding on to walls or furniture when walking around a room, or fatigue from physical tasks such as laundry and shopping. An event such as a fall or accident may be an indicator of decreased physical functioning or may trigger the beginning of a decline in overall functioning. Weight gain or loss may be a sign of altered eating patterns or poor food choices. When individuals have a slow recovery after an illness or a chronic condition which is progressing, they are at risk for changes in their ability to remain independent and should be observed for some of these red flags.

261

Socially, some older adults are at risk of becoming isolated, which can affect their ability to remain independent. Sometimes, social isolation is related to the physical factors mentioned above. An investigation into why daily routines have changed; why the person may be reluctant to leave the house for days at a time; why he/she is not participating in favorite hobbies or interests; or why there is limited contact with previous friends, neighbors, and acquaintances brings the physical changes to light. Mental and emotional factors may also contribute to changes in behavior. If the older adult has recently lost a spouse or friend or given up driving, the grief process may significantly affect functioning. Older adults who are beginning to develop dementia may change their behavior to try to hide their symptoms or may no longer understand how to perform activities they used to enjoy.

There are multiple clues to financial management difficulties. When visiting, look for unopened mail, piles of mail scattered around the house, or mail located in odd places. More in-depth observation may reveal unusual letters from financial institutions or insurance agencies, mail from large numbers of charities, bounced checks or checks routinely written out of order, unpaid bills, or an inability to balance the checkbook. Although many older adults may initially be reluctant to share the details of their finances, the presence of even one of these signs warrants investigation in order to prevent potentially devastating results.

The kitchen is a prime area to check for household red flags to independence. Is there an adequate supply of food in the cupboard/refrigerator, and is it fresh? Are food choices appropriate? Is there an overabundance of a certain item, demonstrating that the individual can't remember what is already in the cupboard when out shopping? Are there signs that the person is still cooking, such as dirty or recently washed dishes? Are there any danger signs from cooking, including burns on potholders, pots and pans that have scorched bottoms or are missing (they may have been thrown away due to damage), or soot and grime on the walls from smoke? Household red flags may be noticeable in other areas of the home as well. Even if someone is able to keep a living room relatively clean, the bedroom or bathroom (especially a master bath) may be a different story. Routine spills which aren't cleaned up may be a sign of dementia. Increasing amounts of clutter should be a cause for concern as well as neglecting routine home maintenance tasks or the care of plants or animals.

One final aspect of independence that should be considered is the ability to drive. Our culture places a strong emphasis on driving as a prerequisite to independence, and, as a result, many older adults probably continue to drive longer than they should. Some indications that driving may need to be monitored include: new damage to the car such as scratches or dents, routinely forgetting to use a seat belt, and unsafe practices such as tailgating or consistently driving below the speed limit. Slow reaction time or changes in driving habits (such as not listening to the radio while driving and avoiding night or highway driving) are additional signs that warrant observation and suggest that transportation support may be beneficial.

These red flags are not an exhaustive list, and a key factor to be aware of is the presence of a change in behavior or habits. Some older adults may recognize their limitations and try to hide any evidence of change, while others have a lack of awareness of the health and safety risks they are facing, affecting both themselves and others. Whether an older adult you know is a family member, a neighbor, or a church acquaintance, your knowledge of their routines, likes/dislikes, and patterns of behavior can help connect the dots when your gut tells you "something isn't right."

Karen Kaslow

OLDER DRIVERS AND AVOIDING DISASTER

Driving is a sensitive issue for many older adults and their families. The Pennsylvania Department of Transportation (Penn DOT) reports that the number of drivers age 65 and older in our state has increased steadily over the last ten years, totaling 1,901,546 in 2015. Age alone cannot be used to determine one's fitness to drive, since the ability to drive safely is dependent upon cognitive and physical skills, which vary greatly among older adults. Due to the highly sensitive nature of driving safety, families often tend to delay or avoid discussions with older drivers until obvious impairment exists, at which time heightened emotions are present, as well as increased risks for both the driver and the general public. An accurate understanding of statistics related to older drivers, signs of potential safety risks, and techniques which can be used to share concerns with older drivers can lead to earlier and calmer discussions which preserve the dignity of the older driver and allow opportunities to pre-plan for changes in driving ability.

People often assume that older drivers are more likely to be involved accidents than the rest of the driving population. PennDot publishes an annual report of statewide crash statistics in numerous categories. Their data from 2014 revealed that out of the total number of drivers involved in car crashes in PA, all of the older age groups (61-65, 66-70, 71-75, and over 75) had a lower percentage of drivers involved in accidents than the younger age groups. These results applied to both males and females. The results may be due in part to alterations in driving habits which older adults often practice; such as reducing nighttime and highway driving, observing speed limits, and avoiding drinking and driving.

However, it is significant to note that when the data was broken down by the location of crashes, it revealed that older drivers are more likely than other age groups to be involved in crashes at intersections. All driving situations require complex skills and quick decision-making, but navigating intersections is one of the more challenging driving tasks. Normal age-related changes, the presence of certain medical conditions, and even side effects of medications can limit the ability of older adults to handle certain driving situations safely and effectively by causing alterations in vision, hearing, attention, reaction time, strength, flexibility, and coordination.

These crashes at intersections are also more likely to result in death for older drivers. In 2013, 45% of fatalities in accidents involving passenger vehicles in a multiple vehicle crashes at intersections were drivers age 85 and older. This is more than double the rate for 16-19 year olds, which is another age group that often is considered to be high risk (Insurance Institute for Highway Safety). The risk of death in these types of accidents actually increases steadily beginning with the 60-64 year old age group. Although we've noted that older adults don't have a higher risk of being involved in accidents, they are more likely to experience severe injuries, medical complications, and death than younger adults, due to the physiological changes that occur with increasing age and the presence of chronic health conditions. This is true for both older drivers and older passengers.

There are numerous health conditions which can negatively affect driving skills. Health care providers cannot "take away" an individual's driver's license. That decision is made by PennDOT. However, guidelines are in place for health care providers to report to the state the presence of certain disorders or disabilities which may impair an individual's ability to drive safely. Some of these conditions include limitations of vision; seizure disorder; unstable diabetes; heart or circulatory conditions which cause

KEYSTONE ELDER LAW P.C.

fainting, dizziness, or lack of coordination; neuromuscular, orthopedic, and other conditions which limit the use of one or more joints or extremities for more than 90 days; and mental conditions which potentially lead to inattentiveness, increased aggression, hallucinations, and contemplation of suicide. Private individuals may also report concerns about a person's driving to the state. When writing to PennDOT, the full name of the driver and his/her birth date and home address or social security number must be provided. The individual sending the report must also sign the letter and provide contact information in case PennDOT has additional questions.

When a report is made to the state about a medical condition which may impair driving skills, an evaluation is completed which can result in the addition of restrictions to driving privileges, the recall of a license, a request for more information, or the need to complete a driver's examination. Medical reporting can also be made to reverse previous driving restrictions or license recall. In all cases, these reports are confidential and the individual about whom a report is filed *will not* have access to it. Anyone who provides a report to the state is immune from civil or criminal liability. PennDOT believes that medical reporting by health care providers is the most effective option for preventing medically impaired individuals from driving.

Warning Signs of Reduced Driving Safety

According to AAA, a typical driver makes 20 decisions per mile and has less than half of a second to respond to changes in the roadway. These factors can be challenging for the most competent drivers. However, when a driver's thinking skills are a little slower, or their physical response is delayed due to changes in health and functioning, this driver may be courting disaster.

AAA and The National Institutes of Health have identified some of the warning signs that older drivers demonstrate when their driving skills are becoming a potential safety risk:

266

- Failing to yield the right of way

- Difficulty staying within their travel lane

- Difficulty in judging the time or distance required to turn safely across traffic

- Failing to come to a complete stop at a stop sign, or missing a stop sign altogether

- Driving too slowly in an attempt to compensate for slowed reaction time

- Driving too fast due to lack of recognition of their actual speed or a fear of being told they drive too slowly

- Getting lost or disoriented in familiar places

- A reluctance to drive alone (having someone else along to be a "co-pilot" is reassuring)

- Other drivers frequently honk at the individual

- Confusing the gas and brake pedals

- Lifting the leg to move from one pedal to another instead of keeping the heel on the floor and pressing with the toes (this can indicate decreased leg strength).

- Signaling incorrectly, failing to signal, or failing to check blind spots when changing lanes

- Unexplained scratches or dents on the vehicle

- More than one minor "fender bender" within a reasonable period of time

- Stopping in traffic for no apparent reason

- Parking inappropriately

One of the quickest ways to determine if any of these signs are occurring is to observe patterns of driving by riding along with the individual on routine trips over a period of time. Speaking with others who have been passengers, or with neighbors who may have observed the driver's ability to back out of a garage or driveway, can lend additional insight into the driver's skills. Observing the exterior condition of the car, the walls and doorway of the garage, and the mailbox may also reveal clues about driver safety.

If an older driver exhibits one or more of the above warning signs, it doesn't necessarily mean that the driver's license should be revoked. An older driver may benefit from taking a mature driver improvement course, in order to learn how to modify unsafe driving habits. In Pennsylvania, those who are age 55 and older are eligible to receive a 5% discount on their insurance rates upon completion of the course. To maintain the discount, the course may need to be repeated every few years. Check with your personal insurance carrier for details. Penn DOT has approved the basic and refresher mature driver improvement courses offered by three organizations: AAA (*www.aaa.com* or visit your local office), AARP (*www.aarp.org* or call 888-227-7669), and Safe 2 Drive (*www.safe2drive.com* or call 800-763-1297).

A professional driving assessment is another option to help determine if an individual is qualified to drive, and/or if there are personal or vehicle modifications which can be made to improve driver safety. In the Cumberland County area, driving assessments are available at Healthsouth Rehabilitation Hospital of Mechanicsburg (phone 717-691-4900) and Penn State Hershey Medical Center (phone 717-531-7105). These assessments vary in length and include an evaluation of a variety of skills in order to determine ongoing driver safety, not just safety on the day that the assessment is completed. An occupational therapist who has received specific training in driving rehabilitation is often the professional who will administer the assessment.

The "Retiring From Driving" Conversation

Initiating a conversation with an older driver about his/her driving safety can create feelings of dread for family members. Not only is it uncomfortable to share with someone that it might not be safe to continue doing something that he/she has been doing for years, but if driving is restricted or stopped altogether, questions arise about how to continue usual routines and activities. New methods of transportation will be needed for maintenance tasks like grocery shopping and physician appointments, but transportation for social reasons is also important for older adults. Feelings of loss may result from changes to driving routines, and acknowledgement of those feelings can help preserve the older adult's dignity.

There are some techniques which can make this conversation a little easier for both the family and the older driver. The content, timing, and method of how concerns are shared will impact the older adult's participation in discussions and planning. Introductory conversations about driving before safety concerns exist can encourage everyone to begin to think about possibilities for handling "what if" situations in a non-threatening manner. They are also a good way to explore individual feelings about this subject, which can then be used to help guide future conversations.

Before beginning discussions about an older adult's driving, family members should do their homework. Firsthand information is essential, so ride along with the older adult on routine trips to determine patterns of driving and the frequency with which warning signs of possible impaired driving are occurring. While one trip may be enough if a driver is exhibiting severe warning signs, often multiple trips over time will present a more accurate picture of the older adult's driving skills. Take into account the different factors which may have an effect on driving skills on a particular day or to a particular location including traffic, weather, the route (main roads versus side roads), the car itself (does the size and design fit appropriately with the older adult's physical size and functioning?), familiarity with the destination, the presence of other passengers, use of the radio, and possible personal stressors such as health concerns. Gathering the observations of others who have witnessed the older adult's driving will help complete the picture.

An additional part of this homework assignment is to investigate potential transportation alternatives. Is public transportation a realistic possibility? Think about the routes and time schedules of public transportation, as well as the older person's comfort level with using this mode of transportation. What is the cost? Where and how is access obtained? Do these factors fit the older person's physical ability, lifestyle and needs? Other alternatives include family members or friends, use of a home care agency or private car service, or the availability of special options for older adults, such as those organized by a local church or senior service organization.

Once the homework is done, consider who is most appropriate to initiate the conversation and how to start it. The chosen individual should be someone who the older adult respects, has participated in gathering the information mentioned above, and can be firm but gentle when sharing sensitive information. Possible conversation starters can include a news story about a driving incident, a general statement about local road construction or traffic conditions, a question about another family member's or friend's experience with changes to driving routines, an observation about a recent event which occurred when the older adult was driving, or a compliment about voluntary changes to driving habits which have been made. The individual should use "I" statements to avoid sounding accusatory, such as "I'm concerned that your arthritis may be making it more difficult for you to drive." If the cessation of driving is being discussed, using the phrase "retiring from driving" may be less provocative than "it's time to stop driving." As much as possible, allow the older driver to express his/her feelings and determine possible solutions.

When a high risk older driver does not recognize or acknowledge the severity of the situation, direct appeals related to safety may help, or the difficult step of removing the car from the premises may be necessary. It is preferable to attempt to gain the individual's cooperation first, if the individual is capable of participating in decision-making and planning. Avoid hiding the keys or lying to the older driver in an attempt to avoid hurt feelings. If an attitude of mistrust develops, that may be more difficult to manage long-term than the initial anger over removal of the car.

When an older adult retires from driving, a decision must be made about what to do with the car. It may be beneficial to keep the car if family members have vehicles which would be difficult for the older adult to get into and out of. Giving the car away may create a stumbling block to obtaining public benefits to pay for care in a nursing home if this type of care is needed within five years of the gift.

For additional information about safe driving for older adults or having conversations with older drivers, Penn DOT has a free publication titled "Talking With Older Drivers" (publication 345), which is available on the website *www.penndot.gov*. The Hartford Financial Services Group also publishes a series of free driver safety guides which are available on the website *www.hartford.com/resources* under the link for the Center For Mature Market Excellence.

Karen Kaslow

ELDER ABUSE AWARENESS

The World Health Organization estimates that 4-6 percent of the elderly suffer from some form of abuse. Exact numbers are difficult to ascertain because experts believe that worldwide, a significant portion of elder abuse goes unreported. The United Nations, in an attempt to increase awareness and combat the issue of abuse of elders, has designated June 15th as annual World Elder Abuse Awareness Day. The significance of this issue cannot be overstated, especially since, according to the U. S. Administration on Aging, in our country alone, the population of those age 65 and older is expected to grow from about 40.2 million people in 2010 to 72.1 million by 2030. What exactly is elder abuse? The National Center on Elder Abuse defines it as "intentional or negligent acts by a caregiver or trusted individual that causes (or may lead to) harm to a vulnerable elder." Following are different types of elder abuse and some warning signs of each.

- Neglect

  A. Inadequate meeting of basic needs such as hygiene, food, and clothing

  B. Inadequate supply of medical aids such as glasses, dentures, medications, and safety equipment (such as a walker)

  C. Lack of supervision of an individual with dementia

D. Lack of care for an individual who is bedridden

E. Unsanitary or unsafe living conditions such as lack of heating/cooling or basic appliances, fire hazards, and home in disrepair

F. Untreated health conditions such as wounds

- Financial Abuse/Exploitation

    A. A "caregiver" has control of the elder's finances but is not providing necessary or desired items for the elder's care and well-being that the elder can afford

    B. The elder is giving away excessive sums of money or purchasing gifts in exchange for care and companionship

    C. The elder has signed documents that transfer property or assets but doesn't understand the purpose of the documents

- Psychological/Emotional Abuse

    A. Changes in behavior, mood, activity level, or daily functioning that cannot be attributed to a medical condition

    B. "Caregiver" encourages the social isolation of the elder

    C. "Caregiver" is controlling, demeaning, or uncaring

- Physical/Sexual Abuse

    A. Unexplained injuries or sexually transmitted diseases

Elder abuse can occur regardless of race, culture, or socio-economic group, and it affects people wherever they live. Several risk factors for abuse have been identified. Women and elders aged 80 and older are more likely to become victims of abuse, as well as those with dementia, mental health conditions, or substance abuse issues. Poor physical health can lead to increased dependence on others and caregiver stress, thus increasing the risk of abuse. Social isolation also increases an elder's vulnerability. Unfortunately, available information indicates that most elder abuse occurs at the hands of family members.

Some victims of abuse may be unable to recognize or speak out about abuse due to cognitive impairments such as dementia. Others may deny that what they are experiencing is abuse, feel embarrassed about what is happening, fear they won't be believed if they speak out, or believe that the abuse is somehow their own fault. Some may choose to endure the abuse rather than face the possibility of moving to a care facility. When the abuser is a family member, the abused individual may not want the abuser to "get in trouble." Lack of opportunity to notify others of the abuse or for others to recognize signs of abuse may occur when the individual is alienated from social contact. Fear of the abuse worsening also increases reluctance to report it. People not directly involved in the situation may not report abuse due to an assumption that someone else already has or will report it. Protecting people who are less able to protect themselves is everybody's business, and the costs from abuse remaining unreported is enormous.

What happens when suspected abuse is reported? Reports of elder abuse (age 60+) are handled by the protective services division of each county's Office of Aging. When a report of suspected abuse is made, an investigation is completed by a caseworker to determine if the elder person needs assistance. The urgency of the report will determine if immediate help is required; otherwise, the caseworker will visit the older person within 24-72 hours to personally determine the individual's situation. It is important to remember, however, that unless an individual lacks the capacity to make decisions, the individual may choose to refuse services, even if those services would be beneficial and resolve an actual or potentially abusive situation. All information concerning the report of abuse is kept confidential. *An important note for everyone to be aware of is that you do not have to have proof that abuse is occurring in order to report it.* The task of proving abuse is the responsibility of professionals. Reports can be made anonymously, although a name may help investigators for contact purposes. Information to report would include your observations and the names of all of the persons involved in the situation (if known). Reporters of suspected abuse have legal protection from retaliation, discrimination, and civil or criminal prosecution.

An awareness of the extent of this problem, the risk factors, and the warning signs are the first steps toward battling elder abuse. We can't allow society's fear of growing old to sweep the issue under the rug. Observe your elderly family members and neighbors and offer assistance to individuals who serve as caregivers to help reduce their stress. Doing so may help save a life.

Karen Kaslow

MISCELLANEOUS

TO KEEP OR TO SHRED?

How long should documents such as bank statements, tax returns, and medical bills be kept? What type of personal recordkeeping should be maintained for tax purposes and insurance, or loan and government benefit applications? Here are some tips to help you organize your files and avoid unnecessary clutter.

What types of documents are important? Let's begin with information necessary to file a tax return. General information would include documents which provide proof of income and expenses. An individual's income is verified by IRS forms W-2, K-1, and 1099; bank statements; and statements from investment accounts. Throughout the year, it is helpful to make notations on banking records for items that are unusual, such as large deposits or account transfers. Notations can help trigger your memory so that these funds can be easily justified to various government agencies such as the IRS or Department of Human Services (DHS). Proof of expenses can be in the form of sales slips, invoices, receipts, cancelled checks, and written acknowledgements from charitable organizations. Documentation of expenses is important if you claim deductions on your tax return. Expenses which are paid by check or credit card are much easier to track than those paid for with cash, so when possible, use one of these methods of payment, even for routine expenses. Accurate documentation can help you avoid an expanded audit and make the process of applying for government benefits easier. A complete listing of information required by the IRS for various credits, exemptions, and deductions can be found in Publication

552 at *www.irs.gov*. The completion of a tax return is best handled by an accountant, but elder law attorneys often use previously filed tax returns as an important source of information when planning strategies to meet the costs of long-term health care. The American Bar Association recommends keeping personal income tax returns, W-2 forms, and all records relating to IRA and other retirement accounts *forever*, although some professionals advocate keeping income tax returns for a minimum of *seven years* before destroying them.

Four years is the length of time recommended for keeping records related to the *sale of an asset*, such as a home or investment. In case an older adult might need to apply for Medicaid, an extra year is recommended as the Department of Human Services has a five year look-back period. These types of records should include proof of ownership and the purchase/sale price of the asset. For a house, keep receipts from major improvements and repairs, appliances, and landscaping. Other records which should be kept for this period of time include business records and items that support deductions on IRS Form 1040.

Seven years is recommended for *purchases and expense bills*; *bank statements and cancelled checks*; records relating to special items such as *educational savings accounts* or the *sale of municipal bonds/treasury securities*; and records relating to *inheritances, large gifts, or lawsuit settlements*.

Additional documents which are important to keep for an extended period of time include *mortgage documents* (for the duration of the mortgage—when paid off, keep the record of satisfaction for as long as you own the property); *life insurance policies* (duration of the policy plus 3 years); *personal health records* (indefinitely); and *medical bills and health insurance premium statements* (5—7 years, depending on whether or not they were used to claim deductions on tax returns). Items which can be shredded sooner include ATM receipts (after you balance your account each month), utility bills (3 months), and pay stubs (only the most recent is needed if each stub includes a payment history for the current year. Keep the final pay stub for each year of employment).

Business and personal records should always be kept separately as well as financial records for individual family members if multiple adult generations are residing together. Although keeping finances separate in these situations may require a little more effort on a daily basis, it is much easier than trying to reconstruct the past. For situations in which multigenerational families are sharing major expenses (such as mortgage payments), a formal agreement which specifies the details of payments (such as frequency and amount) can prevent headaches later on when specific financial information is required for a public benefits application or settling family disputes.

Specifically for older adults: records pertaining to the following items are needed by elder law attorneys when planning for an application for government benefits: *pension and social security statements, documents relating to prepaid funeral/burial arrangements, proof of bank accounts closed within the previous 5 years, motor vehicle titles, the tax assessed value of real estate, and documentation of military service* (by the individual or spouse). Military service documents should be kept *forever*.

Records may be kept on paper or in an electronic storage system. The IRS has specific requirements regarding electronic storage systems, which should be reviewed to ensure compliance prior to destroying paper records. When paper records are destroyed, the preferred method is shredding; this reduces the chances of identity theft. One final recommendation is that family members share with one another the location of important records. Whether young or old, we never know when something may happen which might require us to have the assistance of someone else to manage our affairs. *Keeping records together in a known location* can reduce frustration and save families time and money.

Jessica Greene, Karen Kaslow

INDEPENDENCE VERSUS INTERDEPENDENCE

Independence, or the "freedom from outside control or support" (Merriam-Webster Dictionary), is one of the fundamental principles upon which our nation was founded. Independence continues to be a core value in American culture today, and thoughts of shared decision-making or recommendations of assistance/support from others can send some folks into a tailspin. They will do almost anything to avoid being "dependent" on others. A prime example: someone who refuses to stop driving despite warning signs that his/her ability to safely operate a vehicle is compromised.

Over the years, the general mindset of older adults, their families, and professionals who work with this population has been that the preservation of independence is an important goal for which to strive. Recently, however, I heard a presentation that caused me to rethink this idea. Ken Dychtwald, gerontologist, psychologist, author, and founder/CEO of Age Wave (a company that conducts research and provides consulting services regarding aging issues to businesses and non-profits worldwide), suggested that *interdependence*, not independence, be the focus of society's efforts to meet the needs of an aging population.

What does "interdependence" mean? I believe that its two essential components are 1) a willingness to admit when assistance is necessary or would be beneficial and 2) a willingness to provide assistance to others within the scope of one's abilities. For example, take a dog owner who develops difficulty walking. What is the first solution that comes to mind when the owner can no longer walk the dog and there are no family members living close enough to help? Hire a pet service? Get rid of the dog? If the concept of interdependence is considered, a preteen could be engaged to walk the dog, and perhaps the owner could provide some help with homework or be an after-school contact if the preteen's parents work. This concept is developing into a reality on a nationwide platform in several ways. One example is cohousing developments: projects which include a cluster of privately owned homes or rental units with jointly-owned property and a common house. Residents work together to care for both the property and each other. Some cohousing developments may be specifically designed for older adults; however, they are different from retirement communities because the residents are the owners and remain responsible for all decisions and actions within the development. Other developments are intergenerational, and residents of all ages become an extended family. The assistance of community members can supplement hired help for residents who develop extensive care needs, allowing them to remain in their homes and continue to participate in community life.

Another form of interdependent living is village networks. Participants who live in a general geographic area can pay a membership fee to belong to a "village" or organization which provides social opportunities and helps connect members with needed services such as transportation and home repair. These services may be provided by volunteers or hired professionals. Examples of villages in our area include the Messiah Lifeways Connections Program (Mechanicsburg), the Lancaster Downtowners, and the Support Network at Penn National (Fayetteville, Franklin County).

Projections released by the U.S. Census Bureau in 2012 predict dramatic increases in the number of older Americans in the future. Those over age 65 will grow in number from

43.1 million to 92.0 million by 2060, meaning that just over one of every five U.S. residents will be a "senior citizen". Of this group, currently 5.9 million people are age 85 and older. By 2060, this number will more than triple, reaching 18.2 million. Can you imagine our current policies and systems trying to support this many people? Also, one must factor in that currently, the majority of long-term care in the home is provided by unpaid family caregivers, whose numbers are projected to decrease from more than seven potential caregivers for every family member age 80 or older in 2010 to only four per family member in 2030 (AARP Bulletin, April 2015). Older adults of the future will face an extreme erosion of the available pool of family members who could serve as caregivers.

The above examples of interdependent communities are responses to our society's growing need to find new and creative ways to serve our older citizens. The benefits of interdependence can be financial, social, physical and emotional. In our society, graciously accepting assistance is probably more difficult for most people than providing assistance to others. Instead of fighting for independence at any cost, learning to ask for and accept assistance can help us lead happier and healthier lives no matter what our ages.

Karen Kaslow

JUGGLING MULTIPLE GENERATIONS

One of the trends seen during our country's recent recession is an increase in multi-generational households. Multi-generational refers to households containing two generations (parents and adult children), skipped generations (grandparents and grandchildren), or three or more generations. 25 percent of Americans lived in these types of households prior to WWII, but as of 1980, the number had decreased to 12 percent. Between 1980 and 2006, a steady gradual rise (about 2 percent annually) occurred due to increased immigration and young adults delaying marriage. However, between 2007 and 2009, a 10.5 percent increase occurred, fueled by unemployment and lower income levels during the recession. This type of living arrangement may look inviting for many families who are facing the increasing costs of real estate, health care, and child care. In order to enjoy the financial and social benefits of this arrangement, successful multi-generational households must learn to identify and address real and potential complications and conflicts.

The primary factors for all household members to be aware of are the reason(s) for the arrangement and how long it is expected to last. Is a family member experiencing a life changing event such as the loss of a job, a divorce, a move, or a return to school? Perhaps an elderly family member or young child requires physical care. Some families may decide to pool their resources in order to move to a larger house or a different neighborhood. Understanding the goals of living together and whether the situation is temporary or permanent can help family members develop realistic expectations and provide incentives for resolving conflicts when they arise, which they undoubtedly will.

Does the physical home accommodate the needs and wants of family members of various ages? Considerations for physical accessibility may be obvious (e.g. the individual who is unable to manage stairs). But also keep in mind the availability of private space for each family member and how public areas will be utilized and shared. Families may need to be creative in adjusting physical spaces to suit the needs of several generations, but it is important to allow each individual space and opportunity to continue activities which bring meaning and enjoyment to his/her life.

Discussions about responsibilities, both physical and financial, should ideally occur prior to the merging of households in order to help reduce complications later on. If grandparents are expected to care for young children, the frequency and duration of child care responsibilities should be clearly identified, as it may become easy for parents to take advantage of the "babysitter that is always present." The division of household chores such as cleaning and cooking can create difficulties if various generations have different standards or methods which are not discussed beforehand. Special diets, whether by personal preference or medical need, should be considered. Financial obligations should be clearly understood and respected by all adults in the household so that imbalances do not become a source of conflict. Sometimes, those adults who are carrying a larger financial burden may expect to have a greater amount of control over the household as well. In addition, adults who are unable to contribute as much financially may experience feelings of shame or guilt. Realizing that these types of feelings can influence behavior will help guide interactions in the household.

Routines and boundaries are other important areas for discussion. If everyone needs the bathroom at the same time each morning, there is going to be a problem. When a high school student gets home and plans to do homework, Grandma, who is hard of hearing, shouldn't have the television blaring. A common root of family arguments is giving advice. Older family members may not agree with how their grandchildren are being raised, and all members may be tempted to interject with an opinion during a disagreement between a married couple in the household. Consistent routines and each individual's awareness of and respect for his/her own role in the household can help maintain a calmer environment. Regularly scheduled family meetings can go a long way toward keeping the peace if they are held in an open and non-confrontational manner.

The benefits of a successful multi-generational household can be both individual and corporate. Older persons have voiced that being around multiple generations allows them opportunities for interaction that they might not otherwise make the effort to try, and that spending time with young children helps keep them feeling younger. Grandchildren may be able to learn and share a special hobby with a grandparent, have additional help with homework, gain broader knowledge of their family history, and have an adult confidante nearby when a parent isn't the comfortable choice. Some families may attain a higher standard of living by living together than if they lived separately. The Pew Research Center found that, in 2009, poverty rates were significantly lower for multi-generational households than general households for several segments of the population. Learning to live and work as part of a group develops skills which are transferable to situations outside of the home. These are only a few of the many benefits of multi-generational living.

No matter what the make-up of a multi-generational household may be, the keys to success are communication and realistic expectations. For some cultures, this type of household is the norm. In the U.S., it will be interesting to see if this trend continues to grow despite the fact that the recession "officially" ended in 2009.

Karen Kaslow

SURROGATE FAMILIES AND LONG-TERM CARE

It is always time to turn the page on our bad habits and start new and positive behaviors. Here's a challenge that baby boomers should resolve to do now—reach out with personal compassion and respect to younger people. Interestingly, this might seem to be inverted thinking from the expression "respect your elders."

Over the last century, progress in transportation and technology enabled the settling of our vast country and made the intergenerational family farm all but obsolete. Maybe your children, as mine, are now adults who have relocated outside of our geographic area to fill the labor needs of America's expanding economy. As 20th century labor mobility has undercut traditional family life, affordable cellphone plans appeared in response.

In 1915, a 3-minute coast-to-coast phone call cost $20.70, which was 3 percent of the $687 average annual income. By 1940, that same call cost $3, when the average house rented for only $30 per month. By 1970, the 70 cent cost was the same as a McDonald's quarter-pounder. Now the insignificant cost of a lengthy call and free resources like Skype may deceive us into believing that our family needs are fulfilled by inexpensive communication. They aren't.

Today's communication is not much more meaningful than when I, as a child, chimed in "hello Grandma, I love you" during a 3-minute call. Fifty years ago, Bell Telephone advertised that "long distance is the next best thing to being there." Maybe it is, but it's a "poor second" and an inadequate balm for the loneliness and vulnerability of older persons who are distant from their family's younger generations.

When I was growing up, my mother "adopted" three widows who shared special times with our family. Those surrogates helped fill the void of absent biological grandparents, whom I rarely saw. Until she was in college, our daughter did not realize how lucky she was to grow up in the same town as two sets of grandparents whom she saw often and knew well.

Especially since our children live out of state, I'm glad that my wife and I own long-term care insurance and have colleagues at Keystone Elder Law P.C.. Both will be great assets when aging causes us to become frail, and we need to develop and implement a caregiving plan. It certainly would be a healthy supplement if a surrogate, family-like relationship would develop outside of our organizational environment.

I have witnessed such an intergenerational relationship develop among members of a service club when one is missing a parent/grandparent(s) and another is missing a child/grandchild(ren). Similarly, such relationships can originate naturally among neighbors. Churches that seek a means to translate scripture into practice could encourage and nurture intergenerational surrogate families.

Pennsylvania rewards live-in caregivers. The state initiates an action during probate to recover Medicaid funds paid to provide care in a nursing home. However, live-in caregivers who do not own their own homes and who have lived with an unrelated frail person for at least two years prior to his/her relocation to a nursing home may inherit the home free of any estate recovery.

In his futuristic novel entitled "2030," Albert Brooks suggests that, by that date, the national debt will have outpaced the gross national product, medical breakthroughs with cancer and other diseases will enable longer life expectancy, and older persons will be confined in worn-out and all-but-forgotten cruise ships that are anchored off the West Coast. Young people, who work harder and receive less, will be incited to form gangs and become violent against older people, who seem selfish to them. Could surrogate families be a possible antidote for both the intergenerational separation caused by mobility and the pessimistic clash between the young and old as foreseen by Brooks's novel?

Assimilation is possible - legislature and courts have forced a legal settlement of most of the controversial sexual preference issues. Is Brooks correct that the emerging issue for the 21st century will be the young versus the old? According to a Pew Foundation study, the declining percentage of Americans who are younger than age 15 will cross over the growing percentage of Americans who are over age 65, at the number of 20 percent, just before the year 2030.

How will the legislature and courts manage public resources and entitlements when fewer younger people are available to support the larger number of older people who live longer? Will life-prolonging drugs be provided to the poor? Will Medicare have a maximum lifetime benefit? Will the cost of long-term care for seniors deplete Medicaid funding for young families and children? Will the ethics of assisted suicide and euthanasia be considered seriously?

Politicians have kicked the can of painfully real solutions into the future. Our children will be taxed excessively, not only to repay escalating public debt created by our generation but also to pay for entitlement programs to take care of aging baby boomers. We need to be proactive about this dilemma.

If not out of sheer kindness, then in recognition of your probable future long-term care needs—create a surrogate family. Find younger people in your neighborhood, service club, or church to befriend graciously now. Maybe they will respond in kind, willing to manage and advocate for your care in the future.

Dave Nesbit

OLDER AMERICANS AND THE WORKING WORLD

As a rising percentage of our population, older adults are influencing the American working world in a number of ways. Retirement has become less predictable and more individualized, leading to larger numbers of older adults remaining in the workforce. In addition, an increasing number of younger employees have aging parents, which can lead to these employees juggling work and caregiving responsibilities. A 2014 National Study of Employers sees this new multigenerational workforce as a catalyst for changes in workplace practices. In order to be effective, companies must "recognize that employees' personal and professional lives are both sources of strength and challenges that can affect work outcomes" (p. 56). The employment sector must make some adjustments in order to successfully coexist with an aging population.

For those age 65 and older, the labor force participation rate (those who were employed or seeking employment) steadily decreased from the 1940s until it reached historic lows in the mid-1980s to early 1990s. This trend was influenced by the passage of the Social Security Act in 1935, through which individuals became eligible to receive benefits at age 65. This randomly assigned age developed into an expected and even mandatory age for retirement until 1978, when an amendment to the Age Discrimination in Employment Act increased the earliest legal age for mandatory retirement to 70. In 1986, a mandatory retirement age was mostly eliminated (a few exceptions, such as for airline pilots, still exist).

According to the Center on Aging and Work, several different surveys have consistently found that 70-80 percent of workers age 50 and older expect to continue working past "retirement age." In a 2013 survey by the Associated Press, the primary factors which influenced the decision to retire, listed in order of importance, included finances, health, the need for benefits, the ability to perform the job, and job satisfaction. The desire for additional free time and the retirement plans of spouses were found to be less important. A 2013 AARP study of workers aged 45-74 who planned to work in retirement found that 31 percent of them cited enjoyment of the job as the primary reason for continuing to work, followed closely by 30 percent who cited financial reasons for continuation. Another 21 percent wanted something interesting to do, and 14 percent thought working would help them stay physically active.

While many older workers plan to delay full retirement, situations sometimes arise which can change these plans. A decline in health status is the most common reason that some leave the workforce before they expected to, while changes at their employer (such as closure or downsizing) ranks second. Additional causes of earlier-than-planned retirement include becoming the caregiver for a spouse or other family member, changes in the skills required for work, and other job-related reasons. Fewer people decide to retire earlier for positive reasons such as financial stability or the desire to try something different.

Those who continue working during their older years may choose to stay with their current employer or explore an encore career or "bridge" job. Job enjoyment (80 percent), good work-life fit (76 percent), benefits (66 percent), and feeling connected to the organization (63 percent) are the top reasons given by workers age 55 and older who choose to stay with their current employers (American Psychological Association Workforce Retention Survey, 2012). A "bridge" job can provide an opportunity for some people to ease into retirement through reduced hours and less stressful responsibilities; however, those with or without ongoing financial needs who are seeking a new challenge and have a desire to "give back" may decide to try an encore career. Civic Ventures, an organization which supports career opportunities for seniors, defines an "encore career" as providing "personal fulfillment, social impact, and continued income, enabling people to put their passion to work for the greater good." Marc Freeman, founder of the company Encore (*www.encore.org*), sees great potential in those who are in mid-life/later years, utilizing their talents, wisdom, skill and experience to help solve some of the challenges that face not only American society, but also communities around the world. He states, "It's time to focus on enriching lives, not just lengthening them; on providing purpose and productivity, not just perpetuity." Entrepreneurship is a great example of older workers' attempts to accept challenge and remain productive. Americans aged 55-64 had a higher rate of entrepreneurial activity than those age 20-24 for every year from 1996-2007 (Kauffman Foundation, 2009).

In addition to alterations in how society views retirement, older adults are also influencing the workforce as parents of middle-aged employees. Some of these employees become caregivers, which adds another dynamic to workplace recruitment, retention, and productivity. Are American companies keeping pace with the changes that an older population is bringing? In 2014, the Families and Work Institute (*www.familiesandwork.org*) conducted a nationwide study of over 1,000 employers with 50 or more employees. Its previous study had been completed in 2008. Here are some of their findings.

In general, six characteristics are common among employers who are the most likely to provide benefits for families with older adults. They usually are larger, non-profit organizations that operate in more than one location and have fewer hourly employees. In addition to employing more women than men, they also have more women and minorities who are in executive leadership positions or report directly to these executives. Some examples of benefits include elder care resource and referral services and respite care. Resource and referral services were offered by 43 percent of companies in 2014 compared to 31 percent in 2008. Access to respite care for family members of employees is significantly lower at 7 percent; however, it has improved from 3 percent in 2008. While larger companies were more likely to offer assistance programs, smaller companies (50-99 employees) were more likely to demonstrate the type of flexibility with work scheduling which is beneficial for family caregivers. These companies allowed employees to change start or end times within a general range, occasionally work some paid hours from home, and take time off during a workday (without loss of pay) to address a personal or family need. Flexibility in scheduling work hours and managing the workload, which allows individuals of all ages to participate in the workforce while leaving time for meeting other responsibilities and exploring other interests, has been identified as a characteristic of an effective employer. Between 2008 and 2014, a general increase in employee flexibility to adjust work times without a change in employee workload was noted among all companies. At the same time, fewer options existed for employees who work less than a full-time or only seasonal schedules.

The Family Medical Leave Act of 1993 has had an impact on the ability of employees to fulfill a role as a family caregiver. This act does not have a specific provision related to the care of older adults, but it does allow for "family leave for seriously ill family members." In 2014, 90 percent of employers offered at least 12 weeks of leave for employees to care for ill family members (up from 84 percent). In addition, 75 percent of employers reported that they allow paid or unpaid time off for employees to specifically provide care for older adults without the threat of losing their jobs. Small and large companies were found to be equally likely to offer this benefit, which may be a result of the characteristics of the executives making the decisions. These executives are more likely to be older themselves and have witnessed a similar need for this type of care within their own families.

On its website, The Sloan Center on Aging and Work at Boston College offers case studies of companies that are using innovative programs to meet the needs of older workers as well as workers caring for aging family members. For example, CVS Caremark offers a Snowbird Program in which older workers can transfer to different store regions for part of the year. This program allows them to retain older workers who spend the summers in one part of the country and the winters in another, have workers who understand the needs of their older customers and can provide improved customer service, and adequately staff locations in warmer climates when business increases during the winter. This and other programs which CVS has implemented have increased the percentage of workers age 50 and older from 7 percent to 22 percent of its workforce. Another example: CBS Corporation offers assistance for caregivers through its Eldercare Services program. The program was implemented in response to increased employee absences, stress, and decreased productivity due to family caregiving responsibilities. The program offers services such as health advocates for employees, their parents, and their in-laws to help families navigate the health care system; and back-up elder care, which allows for in-home emergency care for elders for up to 15 days/year at a cost of only $4/hour.

In addition to programs and benefits offered by individual employers, there are a number of public programs which are designed to assist seniors who desire to remain in the workforce. The Senior Community Service Employment Program assists unemployed, low-income seniors age 55+ obtain part-time positions with community service organizations. The National Council on Aging has an online program called JobSource, which offers free training for writing a resume, improving interview skills, and learning job search skills, as well as exploring job options. Family caregivers and older adults who aren't ready for full retirement may still face challenges in locating a career opportunity with a flexible work schedule; however, employers are beginning to take action to support employees who are trying to achieve an appropriate work-life balance.

Karen Kaslow

SHARING LOVE WITH THOSE WHO HAVE
ALZHEIMER'S DISEASE

In one of A.A. Milnes' Winnie the Pooh stories, Piglet asks Pooh, "How do you spell 'love'?" Pooh's response was, "You don't spell it ... you feel it." In order for someone to feel loved, another must share him/herself with the individual. In the presence of Alzheimer's disease (AD), sharing love can become more difficult for both the healthy and the afflicted. As memory fades and afflicted individuals become less able to recognize family members and friends, it can become easy for the demands of physical care to overshadow demonstrations of love. In addition, you may wonder what impact sharing love will have on the individual, since he/she is unlikely to recall the event after its end or even fully understand what is happening during the interaction.

Researchers are beginning to explore the relationship between emotions and memory in people with AD. Dr. Steven Sabat, a member of Georgetown University's Psychology Department, has found that, after a specific experience, people with AD demonstrate emotions associated with the experience even when they cannot verbalize a memory of the experience itself (Mayo Clinic Alzheimer's blog, 9/4/13). Researchers at the University of Iowa conducted a study in which individuals with AD watched film clips about happy and sad events. The participants were rated through observations of their emotions at baseline and at three points in time after viewing the film clips. Their recall of the content of the film clips was also recorded. The study concluded that the subjects' feelings of sadness and happiness lasted "well beyond" memories of viewing the film clips (The Journal of the Society for Behavioral & Cognitive Neurology, 09/2014). The implications of these studies are clear. The emotional memories of recent events in the lives of individuals with Alzheimer's outlast the memories of the occurrence or details of these events. Thus, by sharing demonstrations of love with these individuals, we are contributing to a positive emotional state and an improved quality of life. Although emotional memory remains intact longer than declarative memory (i.e. recall of events or people), individuals with AD do experience a decreased ability in the regulation of their emotions due to changes in particular areas of the brain. They also become more dependent on communicating through emotion when language and reasoning skills are lost, becoming more emotionally sensitive to the moods of people around them. Emotional state, whether their own or that of someone nearby, will impact behavior. When positive emotions of love and happiness are associated not only with special events but also with the tasks of daily living, cooperation and participation in these activities will improve, creating a win-win situation for both the caregiver and the care recipient.

Do you know anyone with Alzheimer's disease with whom you can share some time, attention, and a little love? It may go a lot farther than you would expect. After all, isn't experiencing happy feelings more important than remembering the reason for them?

Karen Kaslow

PREPARING FOR THE UNKNOWN

In this column, we often encourage folks to prepare for undesirable events such as medical emergencies or the development of dementia by choosing to be proactive and utilizing tools such as powers of attorney, advance directives, trust planning, advanced funeral planning, etc. Recently, I received an email from a reader who shared her frustration about being caught unprepared for a situation involving her parents. She lived in a different state from her parents and relied on information provided by her mother, who was the caregiver for her 81-year-old father due to his "forgetfulness" and cancer diagnosis. As sometimes happens, the "healthier spouse" can become debilitated by illness or experience an acute event and predecease the "ill spouse." When her mother experienced a stroke and died two days later, our reader realized how much she didn't know and struggled with basic questions such as where to find her parent's insurance cards and what types of decisions her father was capable of making. The lack of advance planning almost caused an interruption in her father's cancer care. While her mother's death still would have been stressful, our reader recognized that opportunities were missed which could have eased some of the burdens that she was forced to face while grieving.

Not all preparation for the unknown requires the assistance of a professional. Family discussions are valuable, as is the preparation of an estate inventory. An estate inventory is basically a list of all of your important information. If you suddenly were not around or were unable to manage your affairs, what would others need to know? Where would they need to look to find your personal, financial, and legal records? If you don't want to share the details of this information right away, compiling a list of the information and notifying your loved ones as to where the list is located would be an important step toward avoiding potential delays, complications, and costly decisions during an unexpected event.

An estate inventory should include the following information:

Personal: Legal name, address, and telephone number; maiden or former names; date and place of birth; social security number; parents' and children's names; past and present marital information; emergency contacts; health information including diagnoses, medications, Medicare coverage and other health insurance providers, and physician contacts; employment information; military service; and your attorney's name and contact information.

Financial: Note the name, address, and telephone number of all institutions where accounts are located including savings and checking accounts, CD's, mutual funds, stocks, bonds, IRAs, credit cards, insurance policies (life, auto, home, long-term care) and debt (mortgage, loans, etc.). Listed with each institution should be account numbers and the type of account or asset. If you have utilized the services of an accountant or financial advisor, include this information also, as well as documentation of any trusts that may have been established or funeral planning which has been done. Monthly income amounts (social security, pensions, public benefits) and the sources of income are important. Also list any other assets (real estate, vehicles, art, and antiques, for example).

Home: If you are living in your own home or are responsible for utility bills in your place of residence, a listing of provider information is helpful. Include telephone, TV, and internet service; gas; water; sewer; trash; electric; and home security services.

Other: Since many people handle financial transactions and bill paying online, knowledge of login information may be essential to access/manage accounts. Include usernames and passwords when documenting account information. The combination to a family safe and location of keys to any safe deposit or post office boxes should be listed in the inventory as well.

In addition to a summary of the details listed above, your POA or family members need be aware of the location of important documents which verify this information. Examples of these documents include:

- Birth & marriage/divorce certificates
- Powers of Attorney and Last Will and Testament
- Social Security card
- Medicare and health insurance cards
- Stock certificates
- Real Estate Deeds
- Military service records
- Titles to vehicles
- Insurance policies
- Tax returns (previous 5 years)
- Family death certificates

A thorough estate inventory, while it may require some time and effort to compile, is free and can provide your family members with peace of mind that important details about your affairs won't be missed should an unexpected event occur.

Karen Kaslow

AFTERWORD

No book about long-term care should be read as a do-it-yourself manual. Aging adults need support. The best caregiving occurs with teamwork. We hope that a taste of this collection will be an appetizer to stimulate your desire for more information. If a topic that interests you was not included, you might find it to be included among our articles at www.keystoneelderlaw.com. We welcome suggestions submitted to info@keystoneelderlaw.com. We are unable to accept phone calls or offer answers to individual questions from readers who are not our clients.

If you are concerned about a long-term care issue for a Pennsylvania resident who is within range of our office, calling us at 1-717(or 844)-697-3223 is the first step to engage our help. Our primary client, and focus of concern, is always the older person and not the caregiver, unless the caregiver is a spouse. We regularly cooperate with a caregiver who serves as agent for our client; and sometimes our service begins with the modification or creation of the foundational legal documents, which we referenced in Chapter 5 in the article titled: The Basics of Designing and Funding an Extended Care Plan.

Often, our initial counseling leads to a suggestion of how another organization's services could be helpful for our client's situation. We have created a website at www.mypeaceguide.com, which is a comprehensive and unabridged directory of long-term care service providers in the geographic area near our office. Just as an extensive menu is not a replacement for a helpful waiter at a great restaurant, the website tool at mypeaceguide.com becomes more useful after our clients have received our guidance.

If you or your aging loved one resides in a location that is outside our practice area, we encourage you to find an elder law team that is similar to ours. Look for a law firm that employs a professionally credentialed and experienced care coordinator (see www.lcplfa.org). Determine whether the lawyers of that firm make an effort to stay on top of both changes in the law, as well as improvements in the tools of practice. This will be evidenced by their investment to be a member of important elder law organizations (see www.naela.org and www.eldercounsel.com).

We hope that this collection of articles will serve a useful educational purpose to improve your skill, knowledge and disposition. However, there is no substitute for the real value of having an experienced and compassionate guide to explain nuances and to help you to gain access to the best and most affordable resources. There is a reason that the phone number of Keystone Elder Law P.C. spells MY PEACE!

Dave Nesbit

We hope you found this informative. Please feel free to share your experience with others by leaving a review where you purchased the guide.

Made in the USA
Lexington, KY
03 March 2017